JANUA LINGUARUM

STUDIA MEMORIAE
NICOLAI VAN WIJK DEDICATA

edenda curat

C. H. VAN SCHOONEVELD

Indiana University

Series Minor, 1

FUNDAMENTALS OF LANGUAGE

by

ROMAN JAKOBSON
HARVARD UNIVERSITY

and

MORRIS HALLE
MASSACHUSETTS INSTITUTE OF TECHNOLOGY

Second, revised edition
Second printing

1975

MOUTON
THE HAGUE · PARIS

First edition 1956
Second, revised edition 1971

ISBN 90 279 3074 0

Printed in The Netherlands by
Mouton & Co., Printers, The Hague

FOREWORD

The GATE OF LANGUAGES (*Janua linguarum*) is indeed an appropriate title for a series of essays seeking the key to the laws that govern language and its relationship with other social institutions. This name appeals to me, moreover, as a link that connects the modern search with the writings of Johann Amos Comenius, the great humanist thinker in the science of language. His works, like many Greek and Latin treatises from the Stoa to the Cartesian epoch, carry numerous fruitful ideas which now again capture the attention of linguists.

The title of the series refers, furthermore, to the recent past of our science. Nicolaas van Wijk, whose name heads this set of essays, was one of the outstanding pioneers in the inquiry into the structure of language and into the principles of its evolution. The subtitle of his book *Phonologie* – "een hoofdstuk uit de structurele taalwetenschap" (a chapter of structural linguistics) – may be applied to his whole life's work. In 1902, as a twenty-two year old student at Leipzig, he offered a bold contribution "Zur relativen Chronologie der urgermanischen Lautgesetze", published in Paul-Braune *Beiträge zur Geschichte der deutschen Sprache und Literatur*, XXVIII, in which he displays a clear insight into the coherence of sound patterns and their mutations, and some twenty years later he took up and elaborated these views in his first original work in comparative phonology, "Een phonologiese parallel tussen Germaans, Slavies en Balties", *Mededeelingen der Koninklijke Akademie van Wetenschappen*, Afd. Letterkunde, deel 77-79, serie A (1934-5). Van Wijk, and there lies his main strength, never sacrificed the manifold empirical data in favor of a speculative theory, nor did his amazing mastery of the concrete philological material conceal from him the theoretical corollaries.

I am particularly glad to inaugurate the series of essays dedicated to the memory of this eminent Dutch linguist, since twenty five years ago it was he who, along with Antoine Meillet, encouraged my first, modest attempts to grasp the structural laws of language with respect to the factors of time and space (*De nieuwe taalgids,* XXIV, XXV). It is again to the author of *Phonologie* (1939) that I feel deep gratitude for the first support of my initial efforts to dissolve language into its ultimate components, the dyadic distinctive features.

When a quarter of a century separates us from the Prague International Conference, which broke the ground for general phonology, it is appropriate to survey the main problems of this discipline in its present stage. On the other hand, it was tempting to explore, forty years after the publication of Saussure's *Cours* with its radical distinction between the "syntagmatic" and "associative" plane of language, what has been and can be drawn from this fundamental dichotomy.

Leiden, October 1955   ROMAN JAKOBSON

TABLE OF CONTENTS

PART II: TWO ASPECTS OF LANGUAGE
AND TWO TYPES OF APHASIC DISTURBANCES

The first study is an expanded version of the paper in the *Handbook of Phonetics*, initiated by the International Committee for Phonetic Sciences and published by the North-Holland Publishing Company, Amsterdam. The second study is based on the author's essay written for a collective volume *At the Beginning Was the Word*, Harper, New York, and on a few passages of his paper "Aphasia as a Linguistic Problem" from the symposium *On Expressive Language*, Clark University Press, Worcester, Mass., 1955.

PART I

PHONOLOGY AND PHONETICS

BY

ROMAN JAKOBSON

AND

MORRIS HALLE

1. THE FEATURE LEVEL OF LANGUAGE

1.1. DISTINCTIVE FEATURES IN OPERATION

Family names such as *Bitter, Chitter, Ditter, Fitter, Gitter, Hitter, Jitter, Litter, Mitter, Pitter, Ritter, Sitter, Titter, Witter, Zitter* all occur in New York. Whatever the origin of these names and their bearers, each of the vocables is used in the English of New Yorkers without colliding with their linguistic habits. You had never heard anything about the gentleman introduced to you at a New York party. "Mr. Ditter", says your host. You try to grasp and retain this message. As an English-speaking person you, unaware of the operation, easily divide the continuous soundflow into a definite number of successive units. Your host didn't say *bitter* /bítə/ or *dotter* /dátə/ or *digger* /dígə/ or *ditty* /díti/ but *ditter* /dítə/. Thus the four sequential units capable of selective alternation with other units in English are readily educed by the listener: /d/ + /i/ + /t/ + /ə/.

Each of these units presents the receiver with a definite number of paired alternatives used with a differentiating value in English. The family names cited above differ through their initial unit; some of these names are distinguished from each other by one single alternative, and this minimal distinction is common to several pairs, e.g. /nítə/ : /dítə/ = /mítə/ : /bítə/ = nasalized vs. non-nasalized, /títə/ : /dítə/ = /sítə/ : /zítə/ = /pítə/ : /bítə/ = /kítə/ : /gítə/ = tense vs. lax. Such pairs as /pítə/ and /dítə/ offer an example of two concurrent minimal distinctions: grave vs. acute together with tense vs. lax. The pair *bitter* /bítə/ and *detter* /détə/ presents two successive minimal distinctions: grave vs. acute followed by diffuse vs. compact. (For an acoustic and motor definition of the cited distinctions, see section 3.6.)

1.2. STRUCTURE OF DISTINCTIVE FEATURES

Linguistic analysis gradually breaks down complex speech units into MORPHEMES as the ultimate constituents endowed with proper meaning and dissolves these smallest semantic vehicles into their ultimate components, capable of differentiating morphemes from each other. These components are termed DISTINCTIVE FEATURES. Correspondingly, two levels of language and linguistic analysis are to be kept apart: on the one hand, the SEMANTIC LEVEL, involving both simple and complex meaningful units from the morpheme to the utterance and discourse and, on the other hand, the feature level, concerned with simple and complex units which serve merely to differentiate, cement and partition or bring into relief the manifold meaningful units.

Each of the distinctive features involves a choice between two terms of an opposition that displays a specific differential property, divergent from the properties of all other oppositions. Thus grave and acute are opposed to each other in the listener's perception by sound-pitch, as relatively low-pitched and high-pitched; in the physical aspect they are correspondingly opposed by the distribution of energy at the ends of the spectrum and on the motor level by the size and shape of the resonating cavity. In a message conveyed to the listener, every feature confronts him with a yes-no decision. Thus he has to make his selection between grave and acute, because in the language used for the message both alternatives occur in combination with the same concurrent features and in the same sequences: /bítə/—/dítə/, /fítə/—/sítə/, /bíl/—/búl/. The listener is obliged to choose either between two polar qualities of the same category, as in the case of grave vs. acute, or between the presence and absence of a certain quality such as voiced vs. voiceless, nasalized vs. non-nasalized, sharp vs. non-sharp.

1.3. OPPOSITION AND CONTRAST

Since in the listener's hesitation – 'Is it /bítə/ or /dítə/?' – only one
of the two logically correlated alternatives belongs to the actual
message, the Saussurian term OPPOSITION is suitable here, whereas
the term CONTRAST is rather to be confined to cases in which the
polarity of two units is brought into relief by their contiguity in
sensory experience as, for instance, the contrast of grave and acute
in the sequence /pi/ or the same contrast, but with a reversed order
of features, in the sequence /tu/. Thus opposition and contrast
are two different manifestations of the POLARITY PRINCIPLE, and
both of them perform an important role in the feature aspect of
language (cf. section 3.4).

1.4. MESSAGE AND CODE

If the listener receives a message in a language he knows, he
correlates it with the code at hand. This code includes all the distinctive features to be manipulated, all their admissible combinations into bundles of concurrent features termed PHONEMES, and
all the rules of concatenating phonemes into SEQUENCES – briefly,
all the distinctive vehicles serving primarily to differentiate morphemes and whole words. Therefore, the unilingual speaker of
English, when hearing a name like /zítə/, identifies and assimilates
it without difficulty even if he has never heard it before, but either
in perception or reproduction he is prone to distort and to distrust
as alien a name such as /ktítə/, with its unacceptable consonantal
cluster, or /xítə/ that contains only familiar features but in an
unfamiliar bundle, or, finally, /mütə/, since its second phoneme
has a distinctive feature foreign to English.

1.5. ELLIPSIS AND EXPLICITNESS

The case of the man faced with family names of people entirely unknown to him was deliberately chosen because neither his vocabulary, nor his previous experience, nor the immediate context of the conversation gives him any clues for the recognition of these names. In such a situation the listener cannot afford to lose a single phoneme from the message received. Usually, however, the context and the situation permit us to disregard a high percentage of the features, phonemes and sequences in the incoming message without jeopardizing its comprehension. The probability of occurrence in the spoken chain varies for different features and likewise for each feature in different contexts. For this reason it is possible from a part of the sequence to predict with greater or lesser accuracy the succeeding features, to reconstruct the preceding ones, and finally to infer from some features in a bundle the other concurrent features.

Since in various circumstances the distinctive load of the phonemes is actually reduced for the listener, the speaker, in turn, is relieved of executing all the sound distinctions in his message: the number of effaced features, omitted phonemes and simplified sequences may be considerable in a blurred and rapid style of speaking. The sound shape of speech may be no less elliptic than its syntactic composition. Even such specimens as the slovenly /tem mins sem/ for 'ten minutes to seven', quoted by Jones, are not the highest degree of omission and fragmentariness encountered in familiar talk. But, once the necessity arises, speech that is elliptic on the semantic or feature level is readily translated by the utterer into an explicit form which, if needed, is apprehended by the listener in all its explicitness.

The slurred fashion of pronunciation is but an abbreviated derivative from the explicit clear-speech form which carries the highest amount of information. For many American English speakers /t/ and /d/ are ordinarily not distinguished between a stressed and unstressed vowel but can be produced distinctively when there is danger of a confusing homonymity: "Is it Mr. Bitter /bítə/ or Bidder /bídə/?" may be asked with a slightly divergent implementation of the two phonemes. This means that in one type of American English the code distinguishes the inter-vocalic /t/

and /d/, while in another dialectal type this distinction is totally lost. When analyzing the pattern of phonemes and distinctive features composing them, one must recur to the fullest, optimal code at the command of the given speakers.

2. THE VARIETY OF FEATURES AND THEIR TREATMENT IN LINGUISTICS

2.1. PHONOLOGY AND PHONEMICS

The question of how language utilizes sound matter, selecting certain of its elements and adapting them to its various ends, is the field of a special linguistic discipline. In English this discipline is frequently called PHONEMICS (or, puristically, PHONEMATICS), since among the functions of sound in language the primary one is to serve as distinctive vehicle, and since the basic vehicle for this function is the phoneme with its components.

The prevailing continental term PHONOLOGY, launched in the early 1920's[1] and based upon the suggestions of the Geneva school, or the circumlocution FUNCTIONAL PHONETICS is still preferable, although in English the label 'phonology' frequently designated other domains and especially served to translate the German *Lautgeschichte*. The advantage of the term 'phonology' might be its easier application to the whole variety of linguistic functions performed by sound, while 'phonemics' willy-nilly suggests a confinement to the distinctive vehicles and is an appropriate designation for the main part of phonology dealing with the properly distinctive function of speech sounds.

While phonetics seeks to collect the most exhaustive information on gross sound matter, in its physiological and physical properties, phonemics, and phonology in general, intervenes to apply strictly linguistic criteria to the sorting and classification of the material registered by phonetics. The search for the ultimate discrete differential constituents of language can be traced back to the

[1] R. Jakobson, *O češskom stixe* (Berlin-Moscow, 1923, actually 1922), pp. 21 ff.

sphoṭa-doctrine of the Sanskrit grammarians[2] and to Plato's conception of στοιχεῖον, but the actual linguistic study of these invariants started only in the 1870's and developed intensively after World War I, side by side with the gradual expansion of the principle of INVARIANCE in the sciences. After the stimulating international discussion of the late twenties and early thirties, the first attempts to sum up the basic results of the research, Trubetzkoy's and van Wijk's outlines of general phonology, appeared in 1939. The subsequent theoretical and practical achievements in the structural analysis of language required an ever more adequate and consistent incorporation of speech sounds into the field of linguistics with its stringent methodology; the principles and techniques of phonology improve and its scope becomes ever wider.

2.2. THE 'INNER' APPROACH TO THE PHONEME IN RELATION TO SOUND

For the connection and delimitation of phonology (especially phonemics) and phonetics, the crucial question is the nature of the relationship between phonological entities and sound. In Bloomfield's conception, the phonemes of a language are not sounds but merely sound features lumped together "which the speakers have been trained to produce and recognize in the current of speech sounds – just as motorists are trained to stop before a red signal, be it an electric signal-light, a lamp, a flag, or what not, although there is no disembodied redness apart from these actual signals" (1933, p. 79f.). The speaker has learned to make sound-producing movements in such a way that the distinctive features are present in the sound waves, and the listener has learned to extract them from these waves. This so-to-speak INNER, immanent approach, which locates the distinctive features and their bundles within the speech sounds, be it on their motor, acoustical or auditory level, is the most appropriate premise for phonemic operations, although it has been repeatedly contested by OUTER approaches which in different ways divorce phonemes from concrete sounds.

[2] Cf. J. Brough, "Theories of general linguistics in the Sanskrit grammarians", *Transactions of the Philological Society* (1951).

2.3. TYPES OF FEATURES

Since the differentiation of semantic units is the least dispensable among the sound functions in language, speech participants learn primarily to respond to the distinctive features. It would be deceptive, however, to believe that they are trained to ignore all the rest in speech sounds. Beside the distinctive features, the speaker has at his command other types of coded information-bearing features which any member of a speech community has been trained to manipulate and which the science of language has no right to disregard.

CONFIGURATIVE FEATURES signal the division of the utterance into grammatical units of different degrees of complexity, particularly into sentences and words, either by singling out these units and indicating their hierarchy (CULMINATIVE FEATURES) or by delimiting and integrating them (DEMARCATIVE FEATURES).

EXPRESSIVE FEATURES or EMPHATICS put the relative emphasis on different parts of the utterance or on different utterances and suggest the emotional attitudes of the utterer.

While the distinctive and configurative features refer to semantic units, these two types of features are, in turn, referred to by the REDUNDANT FEATURES. Redundant features help to identify a concurrent or adjoining feature or combination of features, either distinctive or configurative. The auxiliary role of redundancies must not be underestimated. Under certain circumstances they may even substitute for distinctive features. Jones (1962) cites the example of the English /s/ and /z/ which in final position differ from each other solely in the degree of breath force. Although "an English hearer will usually identify the consonants correctly, in spite of their resemblance to one another", the right identification is often facilitated by the concomitant difference in the length of the preceding phoneme: *pence* [peňs]–*pens* [pen:z]. In French, the difference between voicelessness and voicing ordinarily accompanies the consonantal opposition tense/lax. Martinet notes that in an energetic shout the lenis /b/ matches the fortis /p/ in energy so that a strong *bis!* differs from *pisse!* only through the normally redundant feature voiceless/voiced.[3] Conversely, in Russian, the difference between lax and tense is a redundant feature accompanying the distinctive opposition voiced/voiceless, while under the special conditions of whispering only the redundant feature remains and takes over the distinctive function.

If the distinctive function of speech sounds is the only one under analysis, we use the so-called 'broad' or phonemic transcription, that notes nothing but phonemes. In a Russian specimen /pil,íl/ '(one) spread dust', /i/ is an unstressed phoneme that includes, furthermore, two distinctive features: in traditional articulatory terms, /i/ is opposed to /a/ of /pal,íl/ '(one) fired' as narrow to wide and to /u/ of /pul,ál/ '(one) took a pot shot' as unrounded to rounded. The information load of the vowel analyzed is, however, far from confined to its distinctive features, notwithstanding their paramount relevance in communication.

The first vowel of /pil,íl/ is a velar [ɯ] in contradistinction to the palatal [i] of /p,il,íl/ '(one) sawed' and this difference between back and front is a redundant feature pointing to the distinctive opposition of the preceding unpalatalized (non-sharp) and palatalized (sharp) consonant: cf. Russian /r,áp/ 'pitted' – /r,áp,/ 'ripple'.

If we compare the sequences /krugóm pil,íl/ '(one) spread dust all around' and /ispómpi l,íl/ '(one) poured from a pump', we observe that the syllable /pi/ in the second specimen contains a more obscure (tending toward a brief, mid-central articulation) variety of vowel than in the first sample. The less obscure variety appears only immediately before the stressed syllable of the same word and thus displays a configurative feature: it signals that no word boundary follows immediately.

Finally, /pil,íl/ may be uttered with a prolongation of the first, pretonic vowel [ɯ:] to magnify the narrated event, or with a prolongation of the second, accented vowel [:í] to imply a burst of emotion. The velarity in the first vowel of /pil,íl/ signals the non-sharp feature of the antecedent consonant; the unreduced, less obscure character indicates that no word boundary follows; the vowel lengthening imparts a certain kind of emphasis.

Possession of a single specific signification unites the redundant features with the configurative and expressive features and separates them from the distinctive features. Whatever distinctive feature, its signification is always identical: any such feature signals that the morpheme to which it pertains is not the same as a morpheme having another feature in the corresponding place. A phoneme, as Sapir remarked, "has no singleness of reference" (1949, p. 34). All phonemes denote nothing but mere OTHERNESS. This lack of individual, particular signalization separates the distinctive features, and their combinations into phonemes, from all other linguistic units.

The code of features used by the listener does not exhaust the information he receives from the sounds of the incoming message. From its sound shape he extracts clues to identify the sender. By correlating the speaker's code with his own code of features, the listener may infer the origin, educational status and social environment of the sender. Natural sound properties allow the identification of the sex, age, and psychophysiological type of the sender and, finally, the recognition of an acquaintance. Some ways to the exploration of these PHYSIOGNOMIC INDICES were indicated in Siever's *Schallanalyse*,[4] but their systematic study still remains on the agenda.

2.4. THE 'OUTER' APPROACHES TO THE PHONEME IN RELATION TO SOUND

2.4.1. *The mentalist view*

An insight into the complexity of the informational content of speech sounds is a necessary prerequisite for the discussion of the various outer approaches to the phoneme in its relation to sound. In the oldest of these approaches, going back to Baudouin de Courtenay and still surviving, the phoneme is a sound imagined

---

[4] See especially E. Sievers, "Ziele und Wege der Schallanalyse", *Festschrift für W. Streitberg* (Heidelberg, 1924).

or intended, opposed to the emitted sound as a 'psychophonetic' phenomenon to the 'physiophonetic' fact. It is the mental equivalent of an exteriorized sound. The unity of the phoneme, as compared with the variety of its implementations, is seen as a discrepancy between the internal impetus aiming at the same pronunciation and the involuntary vacillation in the fulfillment.

This conception is based on two fallacies: we have no right to presume that the sound correlate in our INTERNAL speech or in our speech intention is confined to the distinctive features, to the exclusion of the configurative or redundant features. On the other hand, the multiplicity of contextual and optional variants of one and the same phoneme in UTTERED speech is due to the combination of this phoneme with diverse redundant and expressive features; this diversity, however, does not hamper the extraction of the invariable phoneme from among all these variations. Thus the attempt to overcome the antinomy between invariance and variability by assigning the former to the internal and the latter to the external experience distorts the two forms of experience.

2.4.2. The code-restricting view

Another attempt to locate the phoneme outside the uttered sounds confines the phonemes to the code and the variants to the message. A rejoinder to this view would be that the code includes not only the distinctive features, but also the redundant and configurative features which induce contextual variants, as well as the expressive features which underlie optional variations; the users of a language have learned to effect and apprehend them in the message. Thus phoneme and variants alike are present, both in the code and in the message.

A cognate tenet, advanced chiefly in interwar Russia, has opposed the phoneme to the variants as social value to individual behavior. This is hardly justifiable since not only the distinctive features but all the coded features are equally socialized.

2.4.3. The generic view

Phoneme has frequently been opposed to sound as class to specimen. It has been characterized as a family or class of sounds related through a phonetic resemblance. Such definitions, however, are vulnerable in several respects.

First, the vague and subjective search for resemblance must be replaced by the extraction of a constant common property.

Second, both the definition and the analysis of the phoneme must take into account the logical lesson that "classes can be defined by properties, but it is hardly possible to define properties by classes."[5] In fact, when operating with a phoneme or distinctive feature we are primarily concerned with a constant which is present in the various particulars. If we state that in English the phoneme /k/ occurs before /u/, it is not at all the whole family of its various sub-members, but only the bundle of distinctive features common to all of them that appears in this position. Phonemic analysis is a study of properties, invariant under certain transformations.

Third, when dealing with a sound that in a given language figures in a definite position, under definite stylistic conditions, we are again faced with a class of occurrences and their common denominator, and not with a single, fleeting specimen. Whether studying phonemes or contextual variants ('allophones'), it is always, as the logician would say, the 'sign-design' and not the 'sign-event' that we define.

2.4.4. *The fictionalist view*

According to the opinion most effectively launched by Twaddell in 1935, but latently tinging the writings of various authors, phonemes are abstractional, fictitious units. As long as this means nothing more than that any scientific concept is a fictional construct, such a philosophical attitude cannot affect phonemic analysis. Phoneme, in this case, is a fiction in the same way as morpheme, word, sentence, language, etc. If, however, the analyzer opposes the phoneme and its components to sound as a mere contrivance having no necessary correlate in concrete experience, such an assumption will distort the results of his analysis. The

[5] R. Carnap, "Meaning and necessity" (Chicago, 1947), p. 152.

belief that the choice among phonemes to which we might assign a sound could, upon occasion, be made arbitrarily, even at random, threatens the objective value of phonemic analysis. This danger, however, may be avoided by the methodological demand that any distinctive feature and, consequently, any phoneme treated by the linguist, have their constant correlate at each stage of the speech event and thus be identifiable at any level accessible to observation. Our present knowledge of the physical and physiological aspects of speech sounds is sufficient to meet this demand. The sameness of a distinctive feature throughout all its variable implementations is now objectively discriminable. Three reservations, however, must be noted.

First, certain features and combinations of features may be obliterated in the various kinds of phonemic ellipsis (cf. section 1.5). Second, features may be masked by abnormal, distorting conditions of sound production (whispering, shouting, singing, stammering), transmission (distance, filtering, noise) or perception (auditory fatigue). Third, a distinctive feature is a relational property: the 'minimum same' of a feature in its combination with various other concurrent or successive features lies in the essentially identical relation between the two opposite alternatives. No matter how the stops in *tot* may differ from each other genetically and acoustically, they are both high-pitched in opposition to the two labials in *pop*, and both display a diffusion of energy, as compared to a greater concentration of energy in the two stops of *cock*. How the sameness of a phoneme in two divergent contextual variants is sensed by the speakers, may be illustrated by such onomatopoetic sound reduplications as *cack, kick, tit, peep, poop*.

2.4.4.1. *'Overlapping' of phonemes*

The so-called overlapping of phonemes confirms the manifestly relational character of the distinctive features. A pair of palatal vowel phonemes, genetically opposed to each other by relative wideness and narrowness and, acoustically, by a higher and lower concentration of energy (compact/diffuse), may in some languages be implemented in one position as [æ]–[e] and in another position as [e] – [i], so that the same sound [e] in one position implements the diffuse, and in another, the compact term of the same opposition. The relation in both positions remains identical. Two degrees of aperture and, correspondingly, of concentration of energy – the maximal and the minimal – oppose each other in both positions.

The focusing of selective operations upon relational properties is typical not only of human, but even of animal behavior. In W. Koehler's experiment, chickens were trained to pick grain from a grey field and to leave the grain untouched on the adjacent darker field; when, subsequently, the pair of fields, grey and dark, was replaced by a pair, grey and light, the chickens looking for their food left the grey field for its lighter counterpart. Thus "the chicken transfers its response to the relatively brighter area".[6] It is first of all through the relational rules that the listener guided by the linguistic code apprehends the message.

2.4.5. *The algebraic view*

The approach one might call 'algebraic' aims at the maximal estrangement between phoneme and sound or, correspondingly, between phonemics and phonetics. The champion of this trend calls on linguistics to become "an algebra of language, operating with unnamed entities, i.e. arbitrarily named entities without natural designation" (Hjelmslev, 1953).[7] Particularly, the 'expression plane' of language, as he christened the aspect named *signans* in Stoic and Scholastic tradition and in the work of its reviver Ferdinand de Saussure, is to be studied without any recourse to phonetic premises.

However, each venture to reduce language to its ultimate invariants, by means of a mere analysis of their distribution in the text and with no reference to their empiric correlates, is condemned

[6]   See H. Werner, *Comparative psychology of mental development* (New York-Chicago-Los Angeles, 1940), p. 216f.
[7]   Cf. the criticism of this approach by B. Siertsema, *A study of glossematics* ('s-Gravenhage, 1954), chapters VI, XI, and by F. Hintze, "Zum Verhältnis der sprachlichen 'Form' zur 'Substanz'", *Studia Linguistica*, III (1949).

to failure. The comparison of two English sequences – /ku/ and /uk/ – will yield no information on the identity of the first segment in one of these samples with the second segment in the other sample, unless we bring into play sound properties common to initial and final /k/ and those common to /u/ in both positions. The confrontation of the syllables /ku/ and /ki/ does not authorize us to assign both initial segments to one phoneme /k/ as two variants appearing to their mutual exclusion before two different vowels, unless we have identified the common features, uniting the retracted and advanced variants of the phoneme /k/ and differentiating it from all other phonemes of the same language. Only such a test enables us to decide whether the retracted [k –] in /ku/ implements the same phoneme as the advanced [k +] in /ki/ and not the advanced [g +] in /ki/. Therefore, despite the theoretical requirement of an analysis totally independent of the sound substance, in practice "on tient compte de la substance à toute étape de l'analyse", as Eli Fischer-Jørgensen (1949, p. 231) exposed the troubling discrepancy.

As to the theoretical requirement itself, it arose from the assumption that, in language, form is opposed to substance as a constant to a variable. If the sound substance were a mere variable, then the search for linguistic invariants would indeed have to expunge it. But the possibility of translating the same linguistic form from a phonic substance into a graphic substance, e.g. into a phonetic notation or into an approximately phonemic spelling system does not prove that the phonic substance, like other 'widely different expression substances', is a mere variable. In contradistinction to the universal phenomenon of speech, phonetic or phonemic writing is an occasional, accessory code that normally implies the ability of its users to translate it into its underlying sound code, while the reverse ability, to transpose speech into letters, is a secondary and much less common faculty. Only after having mastered speech one may graduate to reading and writing. There is a cardinal difference between phonemes and graphic units. Each letter carries a SPECIFIC signalization – in a phonemic orthography, it usually signals one of the phonemes or a certain limited series of phonemes, whereas phonemes signal nothing but mere OTHERNESS (cf. section 2.3). Graphic signs that serve to interpret phonemes or other linguistic units stand for these units, as the logician would say. This difference has far-reaching consequences for the cardinally dissimilar patterning of letters and phonemes. Letters either totally ignore or only partially elicit the different distinctive features on which the phonemic pattern is based and unfailingly disregard the structural interrelationship of these features.

There is no such thing in human society as the supplantation of the speech code by its visual replicas, but only a supplementation of this code by parasitic auxiliaries, while the speech code constantly and unalterably remains in effect. One could state neither that musical form is manifested in two variables – notes and sounds – nor that linguistic form is manifested in two equipollent substances – graphic and phonic. For just as musical form cannot be abstracted from the sound matter it organizes, so form in phonemics is to be studied in relation to the sound matter which the linguistic code selects, readjusts, dissects and classifies along its own lines. Like musical scales, phonemic patterning is an intervention of culture in nature, an artifact imposing logical rules upon the sound continuum.

2.5. THE CRYPTANALYST'S AND DECODER'S DEVICES AS TWO COMPLEMENTARY TECHNIQUES

The addressee of a coded message is assumed to be in possession of the code and through it he interprets the message. Unlike this DECODER, the CRYPTANALYST comes into possession of a message with no prior knowledge of the underlying code and must break this code through dexterous manipulations of the message. A native speaker responds to any text in his language as a regular decoder, whereas a stranger, unfamiliar with the language, faces the same text as a cryptanalyst. A linguist who approaches a totally unknown language proceeds as a cryptanalyst until, through a gradual breaking of its code, he is finally enabled to approach any message in this language like a native decoder.

The native or naturalized user of a language, when trained linguistically, is aware of the functions performed by its different sound elements and may utilize this knowledge to resolve the sound shape into its manifold information-bearing elements. He will employ various "grammatical pre-requisites to phonemic analysis" as aids in the extraction of distinctive, configurative and expressive features (Pike, 1947 and 1952).

On the other hand, the question raised by Bloch (1948) as to the applicability of the cryptanalyst's technique to the inquiry into phonemic structure has great methodological importance: to what extent might a sufficient sample of accurately recorded speech enable a linguist to work out "the phonemic system without knowing what any part of the sample meant, or even whether any two parts meant the same thing or different things". Under such conditions, the extraction of redundant features is laborious but feasible in many instances. The isolation of the expressive features is more difficult; but also in this regard the record may yield some information, given the difference between the markedly discrete, oppositional character of distinctive features and the more continuous 'grading gamut' characterizing most of the expressive features. Even a hybrid – bilingual or multilingual – message, as for instance the sentences composed of Russian, French and English words or phrases as used in the conversation of the Russian aristocracy in the late nineteenth century, could be, through the comparison of their heterogeneous phonetic make-up, roughly divided into monolingual sections: "*On se réunit le matin au breakfast et puis vsjakij delaet čto xŏcet*" [õsǝ ʁeyní lǝmątě obʁékfǝst epụí fs,ákǝj d,ęłǝɪt ʃtɔxᵘɔ́ʃɪt], as Tolstoj reproduces the colloquial speech of his milieu in *Anna Karenina*.

A still less manageable problem would be the cryptanalytical discrimination between distinctive and configurative features, especially word-boundary signals, e.g. it would hardly be possible to discover that in such Russian pairs of samples as /danós/ [danós] 'denunciation' – /da nós/ [dǝnós] 'and the nose too', /pagar,él,i/ [pǝgar,él,i] '(they) burned up' – /pagar,é l,i/ [pǝgar,él,i] 'whether along a mountain', /jixída/ [jix,ídǝ] 'spiteful person' – /jix ída/

[jixídə] 'their Ida', the difference between [a] and the obscure [ə], the closed [e] and the open [ɛ] or the palatalized [x,] and the non-palatalized [x] is not a distinction of two phonemes but only a word border signal. Here a cryptanalytical technique runs the risk of multiplying the number of Russian phonemes and distinctive features as compared to their actual stock.

3. THE IDENTIFICATION OF DISTINCTIVE FEATURES

3.1. SYLLABLE

The distinctive features are aligned into simultaneous bundles called phonemes; phonemes are concatenated into sequences; the elementary pattern underlying any grouping of phonemes is the SYLLABLE.[1] The phonemic structure of the syllable is determined by a set of rules, and any sequence is based on the regular recurrence of this constructive model. A FREE FORM (a sequence, separable by means of pauses) must contain an integral number of syllables. Obviously, in Bloomfield's terms the number of different syllables in a language is a small submultiple of the number of free forms, just as the number of phonemes is a small submultiple of the number of syllables, and the number of distinctive features, a submultiple of the number of phonemes.

The pivotal principle of syllable structure is the contrast of successive features within the syllable. One part of the syllable stands out against the others. It is mainly the contrast vowel vs. consonant which is used to render one part of the syllable more prominent. There are languages where every syllable consists of a consonant and a succeeding vowel (CV): in such a case it is possible

[1] E. Polivanov was the first to draw attention to the 'phonemic syllable'. He labeled *syllableme* as the basic constructive cell in the speech sequence: see his and A. Ivanov's *Grammatika sovremennogo kitajskogo jazyka* (Moscow 1930). Cf. A. Sommerfelt, "Sur l'importance générale de la syllabe", *Travaux du Cercle Linguistique de Prague*, IV (1931); A. W. de Groot, "Voyelle, consonne et syllabe", *Archives néerlandaises de phonétique expérimentale*, XVII (1941); J. Kuryłowicz, "Contribution à la théorie de la syllabe", *Bulletin de la Société Polonaise de Linguistique*, VIII (1948); J. D. O'Connor and J. L. M. Trim, "Vowel, consonant, and syllable – a phonological definition", *Word*, IX (1953).

from any point of the sequence to predict the class to which the following phoneme belongs. In a language with a greater variety of syllable types, the recurrence of a phonemic class offers different degrees of probability. In addition to CV, other schemes may be used: CVC, V, VC.

The contrast vowel/consonant is either unique or merely predominant: it can be substituted sporadically by other cognate contrasts. Both part C and part V may contain more than one phoneme, but in contradistinction to C, the part V cannot figure twice in the syllable. The phonemes constituting the parts V and C of the syllable are termed CREST PHONEMES and SLOPE PHONEMES, respectively. If the crest contains two or more phonemes, one of them, termed the PEAK PHONEME (or SYLLABIC), is raised over the others by the contrast compact vs. diffuse or vowel vs. sonorant (cf. section 4.1.6).

The motor correlate of the phonemic syllable has been described by Stetson[2] as "a puff of air forced upward through the vocal channel by a compression of the intercostal muscles". According to this description, every syllable invariably consists of three successive factors: release, culmination and arrest of the pulse. The middle one of these three phases is the nuclear factor of the syllable while the other two are marginal. Both marginal factors – initiation and termination – are effected either by the mere action of the chest muscles or by speech sounds, usually consonants. If both marginal factors are effected by the action of the chest muscles alone, only the nuclear phase of the syllable is audible; if, however, the release and/or the arrest is effected by speech sounds, the nuclear phase of the syllable is the most audible. In other words, the nuclear part of the syllable is in contrast to its marginal parts as the crest to the slopes.

In its acoustic aspect, the crest usually exceeds the slopes in intensity and in many instances shows an increased fundamental frequency. Perceptually, the crest is distinguished from the slopes by a greater loudness, which is often accompanied by a heightened voice-pitch. As a rule, the crest phonemes are inherently louder

[2] R. H. Stetson, *Motor Phonetics* (Amsterdam, 1951).

than the slope phonemes of the same syllable: ordinarily the crest is formed by vowels, while the slopes contain the other types of phonemes; less frequently the contrast of crest and slope phonemes is displayed by liquids vs. pure consonants, or by nasal vs. oral consonants, briefly, by sonorants vs. obstruents (cf. 4.1.6), and in exceptional cases by constrictives vs. stops. If a slope is constituted by a whole cluster, and if within such a cluster there is an inherently louder phoneme in less loud surroundings, its loudness is noticeably reduced to preserve the unity of the syllable: e.g. Czech /jdu/, /jsem/, /rti/, /lpi/, or Polish monosyllable /krvi/ vs. Serbocroatian disyllabic /krvi/.[3]

3.2. TWO KINDS OF DISTINCTIVE FEATURES

The distinctive features are divided into two classes: (1) PROSODIC and (2) INHERENT. A prosodic feature is displayed only by those phonemes which form the crest of the syllable, and it may be defined only with reference to the relief of the syllable or of the syllable chain; the inherent feature, however, is displayed by phonemes irrespective of their role in the relief of the syllable, and the definition of such a feature does not refer to the relief of the syllable or of the syllable chain.

3.3. CLASSIFICATION OF PROSODIC FEATURES

The three types of prosodic features, which, following Sweet, we term FORCE, QUANTITY, and TONE, correspond to the three main attributes of sensation – voice-loudness, relative subjective duration, and voice-pitch. The dimensions of intensity, time, and frequency are their closest physical correlates. Each of these three subclasses of prosodic features presents two varieties: according to its frame of reference a prosodic feature may be either INTERSYLLABIC or INTRASYLLABIC. In the first case the crest of one syllable is compared with the crests of other syllables within the same

[3] See particularly A. Ābele, "K voprosu o sloge", *Slavia*, III (1924).

sequence. In the second case, an instant pertaining to the crest may be compared with other instants of the same crest or with the subsequent slope.

3.3.1. *Force features*

The intersyllabic variety of the force features, the STRESS feature, is a contrast of a louder, stressed crest to the less loud, 'unstressed' crests of other syllables within the same sequence, a difference produced by the sublaryngeal mechanism, in particular by the abdomen-diaphragmal movements, as Sievers and Stetson attempted to prove.[4]

In the intrasyllabic variety of the stress features, the so-called STOSSTON (*stød*) feature, two contiguous fractions of the stressed phoneme are compared with each other. To an even distribution of loudness throughout the phoneme, another type is opposed: the initial portion of the phoneme presents the peak of loudness, whereas in the final portion the loudness decreases. The decline of amplitude, often accompanied by a lessening of the fundamental frequency, is due to an abruptly decreasing innervation of the expiratory muscles, according to S. Smith's analysis of the Danish *stød*.[5] A ballistic movement of the expiratory muscles, opposed to a more even movement, produces a similar prosodic feature, e.g., in Latvian, Lithuanian dialects, and Livian.

3.3.2. *Quantity features*

The intersyllabic variety of the quantity features, the LENGTH feature, contrasts a normal, short, unstretchable phoneme within the crest of the syllable with the long, sustained phonemes of the other syllables in the same sequence and/or a normal, short but steady phoneme with a punctual, reduced, transient one.

---

[4] E. Sievers, "Neues zu den Rutzschen Reaktionen", *Archiv f. experimentelle und klinische Phonetik*, I (1914); R. H. Stetson, *op. cit.*; cf. W. F. Twaddell, "Stetson's model and the 'supra-segmental phonemes'", *Language*, XXIX (1953), and the pioneer work of N. I. Žinkin, "Vosprijatie udarenija v slovax russkogo jazyka", *Izvestija Akademii pedagogičeskix nauk RSFSR*, LIV (1954).

[5] S. Smith, "Contributions to the solution of problems concerning the Danish stød", *Nordisk Tidsskrift for Tale og Stemme*, VIII (1944).

The second variety of the quantity features, the CONTACT feature, is based on a different distribution of duration between the vowel and the subsequent consonant: in the case of the so-called CLOSE CONTACT (*scharf geschnittener Akzent*), the vowel is abridged in favour of the following, arresting consonant, whereas at the OPEN CONTACT (*schwach geschnittener Akzent*), the vowel displays its full extent before the consonant starts.

3.3.3. *Tone features*

In the intersyllabic variety of tone features, which is termed the LEVEL feature, different syllable crests within a sequence are contrasted by their register: higher and lower. The level feature may be split in two: either a neutral register is contrasted with an elevated register, on the one hand, and with a lowered one, on the other; or, finally, each of the two opposite registers, high and low, may appear in two varieties, raised and diminished. When the Jabo people transpose these four levels from speech into drum signals, they use two different pairs of terms for the two underlying oppositions: the opposites high and low are called 'little bird' and 'big bird', while the opposites raised and deepened are termed 'smaller' and 'larger', so that the four signals are distinguished – 'smaller little bird', 'larger little bird', 'smaller big bird', and 'larger big bird'.[6] The voice-tone mechanism has been closely investigated by Farnsworth, who states that the motion of the vocal cords, more complex at low frequencies of vibration, becomes simplified as the rate is raised, until at the highest frequencies of vibration, only the edges of the cords nearest the glottis are seen to vibrate.[7]

The intrasyllabic variety of tone features, the MODULATION feature, contrasts the higher register of one portion of a phoneme with a lower register of another portion of the same phoneme, or the higher register of one component of a diphthong with the lower register of its other components, and this distribution of registers within the crests of the syllable is opposed to the reverse distribu-

[6] See G. Herzog, "Drum signaling in West African Tribes", *Word*, I (1945).
[7] D. W. Farnsworth, "High-speed motion picture of the human vocal cords", *Bell Laboratories Record*, V (1940).

tion, e.g. a rising modulation to a falling one, or both of them to an even intonation.

3.3.4. *The interconnection between stress and length*

Wherever there is a contrast of stressed and unstressed syllables, stress is always used as a configurative, namely culminative feature, whereas length never assumes this function. The culminative function of the stress is regularly combined either with the other variety of configurative functions, demarcation (cf. section 2.3), or with the distinctive function. Languages in which both length and stress appear as mutually independent distinctive features are quite exceptional, and if the stress is distinctive, it is frequently supplemented by a redundant length. The observation of force and quantity features in their intersyllabic variety seem to indicate that the prosodic distinctive features utilizing intensity and those utilizing time tend to merge.

3.4. COMPARISON OF PROSODIC AND INHERENT FEATURES

Any prosodic feature is based primarily on the contrast between two variables within one and the same time sequence: the RELATIVE voice-pitch, voice-loudness or duration of a given fraction is determined with respect to preceding and/or succeeding fractions. As Herzog has pointed out concerning the tone features, "the actualization of the contrasts – given by successive distances between tone levels or by successive tone movements – do shift all the time".[8] Tone level, or tone modulation, stress degrees or its decrescendo (*Stosston*), are always purely relative and highly variable in their absolute magnitudes from speaker to speaker, and even from one utterance to another in the usage of the same speaker. Again, the quantity of a vowel may be established only in relation to the quantity of the other vowels within the context

[8] G. Herzog, review of K. L. Pike, *Tone Languages*, in *International Journal of American Linguistics*, XV (1949).

or in relation to the subsequent consonants (contact feature), while the absolute duration of the long or short vowels in the given language presents a considerable vacillation in speed, depending upon the speech-habits of the speaker and his expressive variations of tempo. A long vowel must be *ceteris paribus* longer than the surrounding short vowels. Similarly, the only thing required of a stressed vowel is to be uttered with a louder voice than the un-stressed vowels of the same chain; and high register vowels must be of a higher voice-tone than the neighbouring low register vowels. But the high register vowels of one, e.g. bass speaker, may be even deeper than the low register vowels of another, e.g. soprano speaker, and in the speech of one and the same person there may be passages with relative expressive lowering of both high and low register phonemes.

A prosodic feature involves two coordinates: on the one hand, polar terms such as high and low register, rising and falling pitch, or long and short, all may appear, *ceteris paribus*, in the same position within the sequence; thus the speaker selectively uses and the listener selectively apprehends one of the two alternatives and identifies the chosen alternative in relation to the rejected one. These two alternatives, the one present and the other absent in the given unit of the message, constitute a veritable logical opposition (cf. section 1.3). On the other hand, both polar terms are fully recognizable only when both of them are present in the given sequence, so that the speaker effects and the listener perceives their contrast. Thus both alternatives of a prosodic feature co-exist in the code as two terms of an opposition and, moreover, co-occur and produce a contrast within the message. If the message is too brief to include both contrasting units, the feature may be inferred from the substitutive cues offered by the sequence; e.g., the quantity of a vowel in a monosyllabic message may be inferred from the relative duration of the surrounding consonants, and the register of a monophonemic message, from the modulation span at the onset and/or decay of the vowel.

The recognition and definition of an inherent feature is based only on the choice between two alternatives admissible in the same position within a sequence. No comparison of the two polar terms co-occurring within one context is involved. Hence, both alternatives of an inherent feature co-exist in the code as two terms of an opposition, but they do not require a contrasting juxtaposition within one message. Since the inherent feature is identified only through the comparison of the alternative present in the given position with the absent alternative, the implementation of an inherent feature in a given position usually admits less variability than that of the prosodic features.

3.5. GENERAL LAWS OF PHONEMIC PATTERNING

The comparative description of the phonemic systems of manifold languages and their confrontation with the order of phonemic acquisitions by infants learning to speak, as well as with the gradual dismantling of language and of its phonemic pattern in aphasia, gives us important insights into the interrelation and classification of the distinctive features. The linguistic, especially phonemic, progress of the child and the regression of the aphasic obey the same laws of implication. If the child's acquisition of distinction B implies his acquisition of distinction A, the loss of A in aphasia implies the absence of B, and the rehabilitation of the aphasic follows the same order as the child's phonemic development. The same laws of implication underlie the languages of the world both in their static and dynamic aspects. The presence of B implies the presence of A, and, correspondingly, B cannot emerge in the phonemic pattern of a language unless A is there; likewise, A cannot disappear from a language as long as B exists. The more limited the number of languages possessing a certain phonemic feature or combination of features, the later it is acquired by the native children and the earlier it is lost by the native aphasics.

3.5.1. *Restrictions in the overall inventory of distinctive features*

The progress made in the phonemic investigation of infants and aphasics,[9] along with the ever increasing number of discovered laws, brings into the foreground the problem of the universal rules underlying the phonemic patterning of languages. In view of these laws of implication and stratification, the phonemic typology of languages is becoming an ever more feasible and urgent task. Every step in this direction permits us to reduce the list of distinctive features used in the languages of the world. The supposed multiplicity of features proves to be largely illusory. If two or more allegedly different features never co-occur in a language, and if they, furthermore, yield a common property that distinguishes them from all other features, then they are to be interpreted as different implementations of one and the same feature, each occurring to the exclusion of the others and, consequently, each presenting a particular case of complementary distribution. The study of invariances within the phonemic pattern of a given language must be supplemented by a search for universal invariances in the phonemic patterning of language in general.

Thus no language simultaneously displays two autonomous consonantal oppositions – pharyngealized/non-pharyngealized and rounded/unrounded. The back orifice of the mouth resonator (pharynx) is involved in the first instance and the front orifice (lips) in the second, but in both cases a narrowed orifice of the mouth resonator, producing a downward shift in the resonances, is opposed to the absence of narrowing. Hence these two processes (narrowed back slit and narrowed front slit) are to be treated as two variants of one and the same opposition, which on the motor

[9] Cf. R. Jakobson, "Kindersprache, Aphasie und allgemeine Lautgesetze", *Uppsala Universitets Årsskrift* (1942) – see his *Selected Writings*, I (1962), pp. 328-401; H. V. Velten, "The growth of phonemic and lexical patterns in infant language", *Language*, XIX (1943); W. F. Leopold, *Speech development of a bilingual child*, II (Evanston, 1947); A. Gvozdev, *Usvoenie rebenkom zvukovoj storony russkogo jazyka* (Moscow, 1948); K. Ohnesorg, *Fonetická studie o dětské řeči* (Prague, 1948); L. Kaczmarek, *Kształtowanie się mowy dziecka* (Poznan, 1953); P. Smoczyński, *Przyswajanie przez dziecko podstaw systemu językowego* (Lodz, 1955). – Th. Alajouanine, A. Ombredane, M. Durand, *Le syndrome de désintégration phonétique dans l'aphasie* (Paris, 1939); A. Luria, *Travmatičeskaja afazija* (Moscow, 1947); K. Goldstein, *Language and language disturbances* (New York, 1948).

level may be defined as narrowed vs. wider slit (cf. section 3.6.3). The relation of the retroflex to the dental consonants proves to be a mere variety of the opposition of pharyngealized and non-pharyngealized dentals. Four consonantal features listed by Trubetzkoy (1939, p. 132 f.) – the tension feature, the intensity or pressure feature, the aspiration feature and the pre-aspiration feature – also turn out to be complementary variants of one and the same opposition which by virtue of its common denominator may be termed tense/lax.

3.6. THE THREE CLASSES OF INHERENT FEATURES

The inherent distinctive features which have so far been discovered in the languages of the world and which, along with the prosodic features, underlie their entire lexical and morphological stock, amount to twelve basic oppositions, out of which each language makes its own selection. All the inherent features may be divided into three classes – (a) SONORITY, (b) PROTENSITY, (c) TONALITY, akin to the three corresponding classes of prosodic features – (a) force, (b) quantity, and (c) tone.

3.6.1. *Sonority features*

I. VOCALIC/NON-VOCALIC

acoustically – presence (vs. absence) of a sharply defined formant structure;

genetically – primary or only excitation at the glottis together with a free passage through the buccal tract.

II. CONSONANTAL/NON-CONSONANTAL

acoustically – presence (vs. absence) of a characteristic lowering in frequency of the first formant, a lowering which results in a reduction of the overall intensity of the sound and/or of only certain frequency regions;

genetically – presence (vs. absence) of an obstruction in the buccal tract.

VOWELS are vocalic and non-consonantal. CONSONANTS are consonantal and non-vocalic. LIQUIDS are vocalic and consonantal (with both free passage and obstruction in the buccal cavity and with the corresponding acoustic effect). GLIDES are non-vocalic and non-consonantal; they never participate in the oppositions grave/acute and compact/diffuse (cf. section 4.1.5), and the basic or only glide of a given language is a one-feature phoneme in opposition to a phonemic zero (cf. Engl. *hall/all*).

III. NASAL/ORAL (properly speaking, nasalized/non-nasalized)

acoustically – presence (vs. absence) of the characteristic stationary nasal formant with a concomitant reduction in the intensity of the sound and an increased damping of certain oral formants;

genetically – mouth resonator supplemented by the nose cavity (vs. the exclusion of the nasal resonator).

IV. COMPACT/DIFFUSE

acoustically – concentration of energy in a relatively narrow, central region of the auditory spectrum (vs. a concentration of energy in a non-central region), with a concomitant increase (vs. decrease) of the total amount of energy and its spread in time;

genetically – forward-flanged vs. backward-flanged. The difference lies in the relation between the shape and volume of the resonance chamber in front of the narrowest stricture and behind this stricture. The resonator of the forward-flanged phonemes (wide vowels, and velar or palatal, including post-alveolar, consonants) is horn-shaped, whereas the backward-flanged phonemes (narrow vowels, and labial or dental, including alveolar consonants) have a cavity that approximates a Helmholtz resonator.

In vowel systems this feature often appears to be split into two autonomous features – compact/non-compact (higher vs. lower concentration of energy in the central region), and diffuse/non-diffuse (higher vs. lower concentration of energy in a non-central region).

V. ABRUPT/CONTINUANT

acoustically – silence (at least in the frequency range above the vocal cord vibration) followed and/or preceded by a spread of energy over a wide frequency region, either as a burst or as a rapid transition of vowel formants (vs. absence of abrupt transition between sound and 'silence');

genetically – rapid turning on or off of source either through that swift closure and/or opening of the buccal tract which distinguishes plosives from constrictives, or through one or more taps which differentiate the abrupt liquids like a flap or trill /r/ from continuant liquids like the lateral /l/.

VI. STRIDENT/NON-STRIDENT (mellow)

acoustically – presence (vs. absence) of a higher intensity noise accompanied by a characteristic amplification of the higher frequencies and weakening of the lower formants;

genetically – rough-edged vs. smooth-edged: supplementary obstruction creating edge effects (*Schneidenton*) at the point of articulation distinguishes the production of the rough-edge phonemes from the less complex impediment in their smooth-edged counterparts.

VII. CHECKED/UNCHECKED

acoustically – higher rate of discharge of energy within a reduced interval of time (vs. lower rate of discharge within a longer interval), with a lower (vs. higher) damping;

genetically – reduced (vs. non-reduced) portion of air to the stoppage of egressive as well as ingressive pulmonic participation. Checked phonemes are implemented in three different ways – as ejective (glottalized) consonants, as implosives or as clicks.

VIII. VOICE/VOICELESS

acoustically – presence (vs. absence) of periodic low frequency excitation;

genetically – periodic vibrations of the vocal cords (vs. lack of such vibrations).

3.6.2. *Protensity features*

IX. TENSE/LAX

acoustically: longer (vs. reduced) duration of the steady state portion of the sound, and its sharper defined resonance regions in the spectrum;

genetically: a deliberate (vs. rapid) execution of the required gesture resulting in a lastingly stationary articulation; greater deformation of the buccal tract from its neutral, central position; heightened air pressure. The role of muscular strain, affecting the tongue, the walls of the buccal tract, and the glottis, requires further investigation.

The difference between tense and lax phonemes parallels that between notes played *legato* and *staccato*, respectively.

3.6.3. *Tonality features*

X. GRAVE/ACUTE

acoustically – predominance of the low (vs. high) part of the spectrum;

genetically – peripheral vs. medial: peripheral phonemes (velar and labial) have an ampler and less compartmented resonator than the corresponding medial phonemes (palatal and dental).

In the nasal consonants this feature is sometimes split into two autonomous features – grave/non-grave, and acute/non-acute – based on the interplay of the nasal murmur and oral release. The pitch of the resonator murmur effected in the nasal cavity plus the adjacent portion of the buccal cavity from the velic to the oral stricture is lower when the occlusion is made in the anterior part of the mouth cavity as compared to the stricture in its posterior part. In /m/ the twofold low pitch is grave, in /ɲ/ acute, whereas in the dental and velar nasals this opposition may be neutralized by the discrepancy between the gravity and acuteness of the two pitches (murmur and release or vice versa).

XI. FLAT/NON-FLAT

acoustically – flat phonemes are opposed to their non-flat counterparts by a downward shift and/or weakening of some of their upper frequency components;

genetically – the former (narrowed-slit) phonemes, in contradistinction to the latter (wider-slit) phonemes are produced with a decreased back or front orifice of the mouth resonator and a concomitant velarization which expands the mouth resonator.

XII. Sharp/non-sharp

acoustically – sharp phonemes are opposed to their non-sharp counterparts by an upward shift and/or strengthening of their upper frequency components;

genetically – the former (widened-slit) phonemes, in contradistinction to the latter (narrower-slit) phonemes, are produced with a dilated back orifice (pharyngeal pass) of the mouth resonator and a concomitant palatalization which restricts and compartments the mouth cavity.

3.7. STAGES OF THE SPEECH EVENT

Each of the distinctive features has been defined above both on its acoustical and on its articulatory level. The communication network, however, comprises a higher number of stages. The initial stage in any speech event – the intention of the sender – is not yet open to a precise analysis. The same may be said of the nerve impulses sent from the brain to the effector organs. The work of these organs – the motor stage of the speech event – is at present quite accessible to observation, especially with progress of X-rays and other tools that reveal the activities of such highly important parts of the speech apparatus as the pharyngeal, laryngeal and sublaryngeal mechanisms (Žinkin, 1958). The status of the message between the bodily pathways of the speaker and listener, the transmitted vibrations in the air, are being ever more adequately mastered, owing especially to the rapid advance of modern acoustics.

The translation of the physical stimulus, first into aural and then into neural processes is about to be charted.[10] The search for the

[10] For tentative moves in this direction, see J. C. R. Licklider, "On the process of speech perception", *Journal of the Acoustical Society of America*, XXIV

models of distinctive features used by the auditory system is a timely task. As to the transformation of speech components by the nervous system, we can, for the time being, at best only hazard what psychophysiologists have intimated as "a mere speculative assertion", sonority features seem to be related to the amount, density and spread of nervous excitation[11] while the tonality features relate to the location of this excitation. The present development of research on the neural responses to sound stimuli promises, however, to supply a differential picture of distinctive features on this level as well.

The psychological study of sound perception has endeavored to isolate the diverse subjective attributes of sound and to determine the discriminatory capacity of the listeners for each of the dimensions of the stimulus. The expansion of this investigation to speech sounds is likely to illuminate the perceptual correlates of the diverse distinctive features in view of their phenomenal autonomy. The initial experiments on English consonants transmitted with frequency distortion and with random masking noise have actually confirmed that the perception of each of these features is relatively independent of the perception of the others, as if "separate, simple channels were involved rather than a single complex channel".[12]

To a psychologist, each attribute is defined through a differential

---

(1952); H. Mol and E. M. Uhlenbeck, "The analysis of the phoneme in distinctive features and the process of hearing", *Lingua*, IV (1954). Cf. R. Jakobson, "Concluding Remarks", *Proceedings of the 4th International Congress of Phonetic Sciences* (The Hague, 1962).

[11] S. S. Stevens and H. Davis, *Hearing* (New York, 1938), p. 164.

[12] G. A. Miller and P. E. Nicely, "An analysis of perceptual confusions among some English consonants", *Journal of the Acoustical Society of America*, XXVII (1955). A fruitful check of the distinctive features on the perceptual level may also be expected from the experiments in progress at the Haskins Laboratories (New York) on the perception of synthetic speech sounds. Furthermore, a cautious study of synesthetic associations between phonemic features and color attributes should yield clues to the perceptual aspect of speech sounds. There seems to be a phenomenal affinity between optimal chromaticity (pure red) and vocalic compactness, attenuated chromaticity (yellow–blue) and vocalic diffuseness, optimal achromaticity (black–white) and consonantal diffuseness, attenuated achromaticity (grayed) and consonantal compactness; moreover, between the value axis of colors (dark–light) and the tonality axis in language.

reaction to a stimulus on the part of a listener under a particular SET. In application to speech sounds this set is determined by the decoding attitude of the listener to the message received and to each of its constituents. The listener correlates the incoming message with the code common to himself and the speaker. Thus the role of sound components and combinations in the linguistic pattern is implicit in the perception of speech sounds. To find out what motor, acoustic, and perceptual elements of sounds are utilized in a given language, we must be guided by its coding rules; an efficacious physiological, physical and psychological analysis of speech sounds presupposes their linguistic interpretation.

3.7.1. *The use of different stages in the study of distinctive features*

In order to decode the message, its receiver extracts the distinctive features from the perceptual data. The closer we are in our investigation to the destination of the message, the more accurately can we gauge the information conveyed by the sound-chain. This determines the operational hierarchy of levels in their decreasing pertinence: perceptual, aural, acoustic and motor (the latter carrying no direct information to the receiver except for the sporadic help of lip-reading and the kinaesthetic feedback). The auditory experience is the only aspect of the encoded message actually shared by the sender and the receiver since the speaker normally hears himself.

In the process of communication there is no single-valued inference from a succeeding to a preceding stage. With each successive stage the selectivity increases; some data of an antecedent stage are irrelevant for any subsequent stage and each item of the latter stage may be a function of several variables from the former stage. The measurement of the vocal tract permits an exact prediction of the sound wave, but one and the same acoustic effect may be attained by altogether different means. Similarly, the same attribute of the auditory sensation may be the result of different physical stimuli.

The theoretically unlikely assumption of a closer relationship between perception and articulation than between perception and its immediate stimulus finds no corroboration in experience: the kinaesthetic feedback of the listener plays an efficient but still subordinate and omissible role. Not seldom do we acquire the ability to discern foreign phonemes by ear without having mastered their production, and a child learning language often discriminates phonemes of adults long before he uses them in his own speech.

The specification of distinctive oppositions may be made with respect to any stage of the speech event, from articulation to perception and decoding, on the sole condition that the invariants of any antecedent stage be selected and correlated in terms of the subsequent stages, given the evident fact that we speak to be heard and need to be heard in order to be understood.

The distinctive features have been portrayed only on the motor and on the acoustic level, because these are the only two aspects for which we so far possess detailed information. Either of these two patterns must give the complete picture of all the ultimate, further irreducible distinctions. But since articulation is to acoustic phenomenon as means to effect, the classification of motor data must be made with reference to the acoustic patterns. Thus the difference among four articulatory classes of consonants – velar, palatal, dental and labial – dissolves itself on the acoustic level into two binary oppositions: on the one hand, labials and velars concentrate their energy in the lower frequencies of the spectrum in contradistinction to dentals and palatals, which concentrate their energy in the upper frequencies – the grave/acute opposition. On the other hand, velars and palatals are distinguished from labials and dentals by a greater concentration of energy in the central region – the compact/diffuse opposition. The gravity of the labials and velars is generated by a larger and less divided mouth cavity, and the acuteness of dentals and palatals by a smaller and more compartmented cavity. Thus, on the motor level, the decisive difference is between the stricture in a medial region of the mouth – dental or palatal – and a stricture in a peripheral region – labial or velar. An identical articulatory difference opposes the velar to the palatal vowels (back – front) as acoustically grave vs. acute. A larger volume of the resonating cavity in front of the point of articulation and a smaller volume of the cavity behind this point distinguish velar from labial consonants and palatal from dental consonants and engender the compactness of velars and palatals. The same articulatory factor determines the compactness of the wide vowels vs. the diffuseness of the narrow vowels. It would have been much more difficult to extract the common denominator of the distinction between labial and dental consonants and velar and palatal consonants or vowels, as well as the common denominator of the distinctions between velars and labials, palatals and dentals, wide and narrow vowels, if the striking acoustical and perceptual oppositions grave/acute and compact/diffuse had not been taken into account.

Although it was evident to observers that among plosives, the labiodental, alveolar (hissing), post-alveolar (hushing), and uvular affricates are opposed by their noisy friction to the bilabial, dental, palatal, and velar stops, nonetheless a similar opposition between the corresponding constrictives was usually overlooked, notwithstanding the fact that all these affricates and the homorganic constrictives are distinguished by a special kind of turbulence due to forcing of the air-stream over a supplementary barrier (the edge of the teeth or uvula) and/or by directing the stream toward the obstacle at a right angle. In the spectrogram, the random distribution of black areas in these strident consonants, as compared with the considerably more regular patterns in the mellow consonants, is the only differentiating cue for all such pairs, and this cue, common to all the pairs in question, reveals a distinct binary opposition.

3.7.2. *Nomenclature of distinctive features*

Traditional terminology resorted indiscriminately to different stages of the speech event: terms such as nasal, palatalized, rounded, glottalized referred to the motor level; other labels (voiced, high, falling pitch, lenis, liquid) referred partly to the acoustical, partly to the perceptual aspect, and even when a figurative term was used, it had some basis in phenomenal experience. Insofar as the feature we define has a traditional term, we use the latter regardless of the stage of the speech event to which it relates, e.g. nasal/oral, tense/lax, voiced/voiceless, stressed/unstressed. A traditional articulatory term is retained as long as it points to an important criterion of division with respect to the sound transmitted, perceived, and decoded. In several cases, however, there is no current phonetic term to cover the feature we define. For such features we have taken over terms from physical acoustics or psycho-acoustics. But since each of these features is definable and has actually been defined both on the acoustic and on the motor level, any of them could with equal right bear a newly-coined articulatory designation such as FORWARD-FLANGED/BACKWARD-FLANGED instead of compact/diffuse, ROUGH-EDGED/SMOOTH-EDGED instead of strident/mellow, PERIPHERAL/MEDIAL instead of grave/acute, NARROWED SLIT/WIDER SLIT instead of flat/non-flat and WIDENED SLIT/NARROWER SLIT instead of sharp/non-sharp.

We are not concerned with substituting an acoustic classification for an articulatory one but solely with uncovering the most productive criteria of division valid for both aspects.

4. PHONEMIC PATTERNING

4.1. STRATIFICATION

4.1.1. *The nuclear syllable*

Ordinarily child language begins, and the aphasic dissolution of language preceding its complete loss ends with what psychopathologists have termed the 'labial stage'. In this phase speakers are able to produce only one type of utterance, which is usually transcribed as /pa/. From the articulatory point of view the two constituents of this utterance represent polar configurations of the buccal tract: in /p/ the tract is closed at its very end while in /a/ it is opened as widely as possible at the front and narrowed toward the back, thus assuming the horn-shape of a megaphone. This combination of two extremes is also apparent on the acoustic level: the labial stop presents a momentary burst of sound without any great concentration of energy in a particular frequency band, whereas in the vowel /a/ there is no strict limitation of time, and the energy is concentrated in a relatively narrow region of maximum aural sensitivity. In the first constituent, there is an extreme limitation in the time domain but no ostensible limitation in the frequency domain, whereas the second constituent shows no ostensible limitation in the time domain but a maximum limitation in the frequency domain. Consequently, the diffuse stop with its maximal reduction in the energy output offers the closest approach to silence, while the open vowel represents the highest energy output of which the human vocal apparatus is capable.

This polarity between the minimum and the maximum of energy appears primarily as a CONTRAST between two successive units –

the optimal consonant and the optimal vowel. Thus the elementary phonemic frame, the syllable, is established. Since many languages lack syllables without a prevocalic consonant and/or with a post-vocalic consonant, CV (Consonant + Vowel) proves to be the only universal model of the syllable.

4.1.2. *The role of the nasal consonant*

The choice between /pa/ and /a/ and/or /pa/ and /ap/, may become the first carrier of meaning in the very early stages of child language. Usually, however, the infant preserves for a time a constant syllable scheme and splits both constituents of this syllable, first the consonant and later the vowel, into distinctive alternatives.

Most frequently, the oral stop, utilizing a single closed tract, obtains a counterpart in the nasal consonant, which combines a closed main tract with an open subsidiary tract and thereby supplements the specific traits of a stop with a secondary vocalic characteristic. Before there appeared the consonantal opposition nasal/ oral, consonant was distinguished from vowel as closed tract from open tract. Once the nasal consonant has been opposed to the oral as presence to absence of the open tract, the contrast consonant/ vowel is revalued as presence vs. absence of a closed tract.

Various further oppositions, modifying and attenuating the primary optimal contrast of consonant and vowel, follow. All these later formations reshape the mouth resonator in some way, while nasalization merely adds a secondary resonating cavity to the mouth resonator without changing its volume and shape.

The consonantal opposition nasal/oral, which belongs to the earliest acquisitions of the child, is ordinarily the most resistant opposition of consonants in aphasia, and it occurs in all the languages of the world except for some scarce American Indian languages.

4.1.3. *The primary triangle*

The opposition nasal vs. oral stop, however, may be preceded by the split of the stop into two opposites, labial and dental. After the

appearance of the contrast CV, founded upon one attribute of
sound, loudness, the utilization of the other basic attribute, pitch,
is psychologically inferable. Thus the first tonality opposition is
instituted: grave/acute, in other words, the concentration of energy
in the lower vs. upper frequencies of the spectrum. In /p/ the lower
end predominates, while in /t/ the upper is the stronger one. It is
quite natural that the first tonality feature should affect not the
vowel /a/, with its maximal concentration of energy in a narrow
central region of the spectrum, but the consonant /p/, with its
maximal diffusion of energy over a wide frequency band.

At this stage the pole of high and concentrated energy /a/ contrasts with the low energy stops /p/ and /t/. Both stops are opposed
to each other by a predominance of one or the other end of the
frequency spectrum, as the gravity and acuteness poles. These two
dimensions underlie a TRIANGULAR pattern of phonemes (or at
least of oral phonemes if the nasality feature has already emerged):

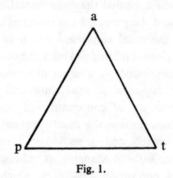

Fig. 1.

4.1.4. *The split of the primary triangle into two triangles, consonantal and vocalic*

The rise of the consonantal tonality feature is followed by the first
vocalic split. The polarity of two successive units, CV, based on
the contrast of reduced and full energy is supplemented by a
polarity of two alternative vowels, founded on the opposition of

lower and higher concentration of energy. The single compact /a/ finds its opposite in a diffuse vowel. Henceforth, both the consonantal and the vocalic section of the primary triangle construct each its own linear pattern – the grave/acute consonantal axis and the compact/diffuse vocalic axis. The consonants duplicate this originally vocalic opposition, and the consonantal base-line of the overall triangle is complemented by a consonantal apex – the velar stop that Grimm had already justly defined as the "fullest of all producible consonants".

The tonality opposition, originally consonantal, may in turn be extended to the vocalic pattern: it is naturally the diffuse vowel that splits into grave and acute, complementing the vocalic apex of the overall triangle by a /u/ – /i/ base-line. In this way the originally single primary triangle is partitioned into two autonomous two-dimensional patterns – the consonantal and the vocalic triangle:

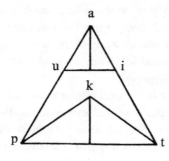

Fig. 2.

4.1.5. *Patterning of oral resonance features*

Both the vocalic and the consonantal pattern may subsequently pass from the triangular to the quadrangular pattern by superimposing the distinction between velar and palatal upon the wide vowels and/or upon the consonants. In this way the grave/acute feature spreads to the compact vowels and/or consonants. In the languages of the world, however, the triangular pattern prevails over the quadrangular for vowels and even more so for consonants: it is the minimum model, both for the vocalic and for the consonantal patterns, with the very rare exceptions in which either the vocalic or the consonantal pattern – but never both – is linear. In the rare cases of a linear patterning, the vowels are confined to the feature compact/diffuse and the consonants, almost unfailingly, to the tonality feature. Thus no language lacks the oppositions grave/acute and compact/diffuse, whereas any other opposition may be absent in the systems of vowels and consonants.

The alternation in the volume and shape of the mouth resonator is used for the grave/acute opposition. In the early stages of child language, in the advanced stages of aphasia and in numerous languages of the world, this alternation is reinforced by the variation in the size of one or both orifices of the mouth cavity. The restriction of the back and front orifices, together with an expanded and unified oral cavity, serve to lower the resonance frequencies, whereas the combined action of the dilated orifices and of a restricted and compartmented cavity raise the resonance frequencies. But the change in the size of each of these orifices may achieve an autonomous status and set in operation secondary tonality features (flatting and/or sharping).

The development of the oral resonance features in child language presents a whole chain of successive acquisitions interlinked by laws of implication. We tentatively tabulate this temporal series in the following chart, using for the distinctions acquired the traditional articulatory terms and designating each of these acquisitions by a sequence of numbers preceded by 0., i.e. writing each sequence as a decimal fraction. The sequences were composed in such a way that if sequence S_1 is assigned to distinction A and sequence S_2 to distinction B, and S_1 is an initial subsequence of S_2 (i.e. S_1 is an initial subsequence of S_2 if the first digits of S_2 are identical with S_1; e.g. $S_1 = 0.19$ and $S_2 = 0.195$), then the acquisition of distinction B implies that of A. The number and numerical values of the digits have no other significance. It is obvious that only those distinctions are acquired by the child which are present in the language being learned.

Consonants: dental vs. labial 0.1
Vowels: narrow vs. wide 0.11
Narrow vowels: palatal vs. velar 0.111
Wide vowels: palatal vs. velar 0.1111
Narrow palatal vowels: rounded vs. unrounded 0.1112
Wide palatal vowels: rounded vs. unrounded 0.11121
Velar vowels: unrounded vs. rounded 0.1113
Consonants: velopalatal vs. labial and dental 0.112
Consonants: palatal vs. velar 0.1121
Consonants: rounded vs. unrounded or
           pharyngealized vs. non-pharyngealized . . 0.1122
Consonants: palatalized vs. non-palatalized 0.1123

4.1.6. *Sonority features in relation to the optimal consonant and vowel*

The reduced concentration of energy in the diffuse vowel moves it away from the optimal, compact vowel in the direction toward the consonants and, conversely, the reduced spread of energy in the compact consonant diverts it from the optimal, diffuse consonant in the direction towards the vowel.

In the nasal consonants the addition of the new, open resonator superimposes sharply-defined nasal formants upon the spectrum of the oral stop. Nasal resonance brings consonants closer to vowels and, on the other hand, when superimposed upon a vocalic spectrum, damps the other formants and deflects the vowel from its optimal pattern.

The optimal, stop consonant finds its opposite in the constrictive that attenuates the consonantal reduction of energy. Stops are an earlier acquisition of children and a later loss of aphasics than constrictive phonemes. There are several languages in the world without constrictives but no languages without stops.

The appearance of liquids which combine the clear-cut formant structure of a vowel with the consonantal reduction of energy, changes the contrast consonant/vowel into two autonomous oppositions, consonantal/non-consonantal and vocalic/non-vocalic.

While the consonantal feature, reduction of energy, is optimally represented by the stop which tends toward a single pulse, the non-vocalic feature, absence of sharply-defined formant structure, is optimally manifested by the strident consonant which tends towards white noise. Therefore, the mutual emancipation of the two features, abrupt/continuant on the one hand, and strident/mellow on the other, implies the acquisition of a liquid that combines two autonomous features, the vocalic and the consonantal. Actually, mellow constrictives opposed to strident constrictives, or strident plosives (affricates) opposed to mellow plosives (stops proper) do not appear in child language before the emergence of the first liquid, and in aphasia, vanish when the liquids are lost.

Strident plosives, in contradistinction to mellow plosives, attenuate the consonantal reduction of energy. The mellow constrictives deviate from the non-vocalic optimum embodied in the strident constrictives, namely from their markedly noisy pattern. One and the same split of the consonantal feature, on the one hand, and of the non-vocalic feature, on the other, is manifested both in the appearance of the liquids and of the strident stops. This explains the 'strange but widespread' interchangeability of strident stops and liquids, especially laterals, that have been noted in Manchu-Tungus and in Paleosiberian languages.[1]

Since nasality, by superimposing a clear-cut formant structure upon the consonantal pattern, brings consonants closer to vowels, and since liquids combine the consonantal with the vocalic feature, it is advantageous to range these two related classes of phonemes under a common heading of SONORANTS. The consonantal character of these two classes is again reinforced in such relatively rare phonemes as the abrupt nasals (the so-called prenasalized stops) and the strident liquids (the sibilant laterals or vibrants).

The oral phonemes with an obstructed buccal tract have a noise source at the obstruction and may use voice – if ever – only as a supplementary source, whereas for the phonemes with an open tract, the voice is the main source. While the optimal consonant is voiceless and the optimal vowel voiced, the voicing of

[1] K. Bouda, "Lateral and Sibilant", *Zeitschrift für Phonetik*, I (1947).

consonants or, in very rare instances, the unvoicing of vowels, may be utilized as one of the various phonemic attenuations of the maximum contrast CV.

Since the consonant is primarily characterized by reduction of energy, the optimal consonant is lax but may be subsequently opposed by a tense consonant that attenuates the contrast between consonant and vowel. Normally, however, the voiced consonant is of lower energy than the voiceless and therefore, in the opposition of tense and lax consonants, the laxness is frequently accompanied by voicing and the tenseness, by voicelessness, so that the consonant, optimal in one respect – reduction of energy – deviates from the consonantal optimum in another way – the presence of voice. If both oppositions act autonomously in a language, the doubly optimal consonant, lax and voiceless, is opposed by two phonemes, one, a voiceless tense and the other, a voiced lax, both of which, though in different ways, shift the structure of the consonant toward that of the vowel. A further move in this direction is a consonant endowed with the distinctive features of tenseness and voicing, such as /dʻ/ in some languages of India.

Normally, the total energy of a vowel increases along with the concentration of energy (compactness), but in a tense vowel, as compared with the corresponding lax vowel, the total energy increases, whereas the concentration of energy decreases. This reversal separates the tense vowels from the vocalic optimum.

While reducing the time, the checked consonants increase their energy and thus attenuate the consonantal optimum. If a language possesses the two oppositions, checked/unchecked and tense/lax, then the optimal consonant, lax and unchecked, is opposed by two phonemes, the one checked (namely ejective), the other tense. A double attenuation of the consonantal optimum may be further presented by the rare combination of two distinctive features, tense and checked within one and same phoneme, such as the Avar /K'/.

Thus, on the one hand, those oppositions which bear upon the SONORITY and PROTENSITY AXES display various fissions and attenuations of the primary contrast between the optimal consonant and the optimal vowel, and thus give rise to more minute and specific distinctions. On the other hand, those oppositions that involve the TONALITY AXES, perpendicular to the sonority axis, emerge originally as the counterpart and corollary of the contrast, 'optimal vowel vs. optimal consonant' and, subsequently, as the corollary of the opposition, 'optimal, compact vowel vs. attenuated, diffuse vowel' or 'optimal, diffuse consonant vs. attenuated, compact consonant'.

4.2. THE DICHOTOMOUS SCALE

In their recent, quite autonomous development, phonemic analysis and the mathematical theory of communication arrived at fundamentally similar and mutually complementary conclusions, making possible most productive cooperation on both sides. Any spoken message presents the listener with two complementary alignments of information: on the one hand the chain of phonemes yields sequentially encoded information, on the other hand every phoneme is composed of several distinctive features. The totality of these features is the minimum number of binary selections necessary for the specification of any given phoneme. In reducing the phonemic information contained in the sequence to the smallest number of alternatives, we find the most economical and, consequently, the optimal solution: the minimum number of the simplest operations would suffice to encode and decode the whole message. When analyzing a given language into its ultimate constituents, we seek the smallest set of distinctive oppositions which enable us to identify each phoneme of the messages framed in this language. This task requires an isolation of distinctive features from concurrent or adjoining redundant features.

If in a language, one and the same phoneme is implemented as a palatal stop before /i/, as a post-alveolar affricate before /e/ and as a velar stop in all other positions, the invariant must be determined as a compact (forward-flanged) consonant, distinct from the diffuse (backward-flanged) consonants /p/ and /t/ of the same language. While, in such a case, the redundant features are conditioned by the different distinctive features of the following phoneme, a striking example of redundant features linked to concurrent distinctive features may be found in the French consonantal pattern. Here, the compactness of the consonant is implemented by a velar articulation when lumped with plosiveness in /k/ and /g/, by a palatal articulation when lumped with nasality in /ɲ/, and by a post-alveolar articulation when lumped with constrictiveness in /ʃ/ and /ʒ/.

Such a delimitation of distinctive and redundant features not only permits an identification of all the phonemes involved but is the unique solution, since any different analysis of these five phonemes deviates from the optimal solution. The fifteen French consonant phonemes under consideration require only five binary decisions: nasal/oral, and if oral then continuant/abrupt, and tense/lax; compact/diffuse, and if diffuse then grave/acute. Each French consonant contains from two (compact nasal) to five distinctive features. If one deems the point of articulation distinctive, and the difference between constrictive and stop redundant, then the six French voiceless consonants – velar /k/, post-alveolar /ʃ/, alveolar /s/, dental /t/, labiodental /f/ and bilabial /p/ – would require, for their identification, fifteen distinctions instead of three, according to the elementary mathematical formula cited by Twaddell: "If x is the maximum number of significant phonological differentiations within a given articulatory range in a language, then $2x = n(n-1)$, where n is the maximum number of phonemes in that range." Some of the minute differences in the point of articulation have, moreover, the disadvantage of being by themselves hardly recognizable for the listener. Finally, such distinctions as /s/ vs. /f/ and /t/ vs. /p/ offer an identical differential criterion, namely the opposition of an acute and grave consonant due to the same difference in the size and shape of the mouth resonator. Again /k/ vs. /t/ and /ʃ/ vs. /s/ display (acoustically as well as genetically) one and the same opposition, based on a parallel relation of the front and back resonators, so that the aprioristic operation with both pairs, as if they were distinguished by two separate features, introduces superfluous redundancies.

The reduction of language into distinctive features must be

consistent. If, for instance, the Czech /l/, which can occur in identical positions with each of the 32 other phonemes of the language, is declared 'an unanalyzable distinctive unit', its distinction from the other 32 phonemes would require 32 unanalyzable relations, whereas through the dissolution of the *l* bundle into the three constituent features – vocalic, consonantal, and continuous – its relation to all other phonemes of the pattern is reduced to three binary selections.

The maximum elimination of redundancies and the minimum number of distinctive alternatives is a principle that permits an affirmative answer to the focal question raised by Chao already in 1934 as to whether the task of breaking down a given language into its ultimate components yields a unique solution. Not less crucial is his later question, whether the dichotomous scale is an expedient principle which the analyzer can profitably impose upon the linguistic code, or whether this scale is inherent in the structure of language.[2] There are several weighty arguments in favor of the latter solution.

First, a system of distinctive features based on a mutually implicating relation between the terms of each binary opposition is the optimal code, and it is unwarranted to assume that the speech participants use a more complicated and less economical set of differential criteria in their encoding and decoding operations. Recent experiments have confirmed that multi-dimensional auditory displays are most easily learned and perceived when 'binary-coded'.[3]

Second, the phonemic code is acquired in the earliest years of childhood and, as psychology reveals, in a child's mind the pair is anterior to isolated objects.[4] The binary opposition is a child's first logical operation. Both opposites arise simultaneously and force

---

[2]   Y. R. Chao, review of Jakobson, Fant, Halle, *Preliminaries ...*, in *Romance Philology*, VIII (1954).

[3]   I. Pollack and L. Ficks, "Information of elementary multi-dimensional auditory displays", *Journal of the Acoustical Society of America*, XXVI (1954).

[4]   See H. Wallon, *Les origines de la pensée chez l'enfant*, I (Paris, 1945). For the pivotal role of gradual binary fissions in child development, cf. T. Parsons and R. F. Bales, *Family, socialization and interaction process* (Glencoe, 1955).

the infant to choose one and to suppress the other of the two alternatives.

Third, almost all of the distinctive features show an unquestionably dichotomous structure on their acoustic and, correspondingly, on their motor level. Among the features of the vowel pattern, only the distinction compact/diffuse often presents a higher number of terms, mostly three. For example, /æ/ is to /e/ as /e/ is to /i/: the geometric mean /e/ is non-compact in relation to /æ/ and non-diffuse in relation to /i/ (cf. section 3.6.1). Psychological experiments that obtained /e/ through the mixture of /æ/ and /i/, confirm the peculiar structure of this vocalic feature.[5] Parallel experiments in mixing vowels situated on the tonality axis showed that grave and acute vowels, when sounded simultaneously, are not perceived as a single vowel: /u/ and /i/ merge neither into /y/ nor into /ü/. The vocalic feature grave/acute is a patently binary opposition.

Similarly, the effort to project the vocalic oppositions tense/lax and compact/diffuse upon one and the same line is hampered by the salient difference between their physical essence,[6] by the dissimilar parts they play in linguistic structure and by the considerable disadvantages which their unidimensional treatment imposes upon the analysis.

Finally, the application of the dichotomous scale makes the stratified structure of the phonemic patterns, their governing laws of implication, and the consequent typology of languages so transparent that the inherence of this scale in the linguistic system is quite manifest.

4.3. THE SPATIO-TEMPORAL PATTERN
OF PHONEMIC OPERATIONS

If there is a difference between the linguistic patterns of two speech

---

[5]   See K. Huber, "Die Vokalmischung und das Qualitätensystem der Vokale", *Archiv für Psychologie*, XCI (1934).
[6]   See especially L. Barczinski and E. Thienhaus, "Klangspektren und Lautstärke deutscher Sprachlaute", *Archives néerlandaises de phonétique expérimentale*, XI (1935).

communities, interlocution between members of the two communities demands an adjustment of the listener to the speaker and/ or of the speaker to the listener. This adjustment may involve all aspects of language or only a few of them. Sometimes the phonemic code is the only one affected. Both on the listener's and on the speaker's side there are different degrees of this adjustment process, aptly called CODE SWITCHING by communication engineers. The receiver trying to understand the sender, and/or the sender in trying to make himself understood, concentrate their attention on the common core of their codes. A higher degree of adjustment is displayed in the effort to overcome the phonemic differences by switching rules, which increase the intelligibility of the message for its addressee. Having found these cues, the interlocutor may try to use them not only as a listener, but also more actively, in adapting his own utterances to the pattern of his addressee.

The phonemic adjustment may cover the whole lexical stock, or the imitation of the neighbor's phonemic code may be confined to a certain set of words directly borrowed from the neighbor or at least particularly stamped by his use of them. Whatever the adjustments are, they help the speaker to increase the radius of communication, and if often practiced, they are likely to enter into his everyday language. Under favorable circumstances they may subsequently infiltrate into the general use of the speech community, either as a particular speech fashion or as a new pattern fully substituted for the former norm. Interdialectal communication and its influence on intradialectal communication must be analyzed from a linguistic and, particularly, from a phonological point of view.

The problem of bridging space stops neither at the borders of distant and highly differentiated dialects, nor at the boundaries of cognate or even unrelated languages. Mediators, more or less bilingual, adapt themselves to the foreign phonemic code. Their prestige grows with the widening radius of their audience and may further a diffusion of their innovations among their monolingual tribesmen.

Not only interdialectal, but also the interlingual adjustment may affect the phonemic code without limitation to borrowed words or even without any lexical borrowing. In all parts of the world, linguists have been surprised, as Sapir confesses, to observe "the remarkable fact that distinctive phonetic features tend to be distributed over wide areas regardless of the vocabularies and structures of the language involved" (1949, p. 25). This far-reaching phenomenon still awaits systematic mapping and study in connection with the equally urgent inquiry into the typology of phonemic patterns.

The other possibility of phonemic adjustment to a different dialect or foreign language is a partial or total preservation of its phonemic structure in borrowed words. As insistently noted by Mathesius (see Vachek, 1964) and closely examined by Fries and Pike (1949), "the speech of monolingual natives of some languages is comprised of more than one phonemic system". Such a coexistence of two systems within one language is due either to a phonemic difference between the original vocabulary and unassimilated loan words, or to the use of two patterns, one native and the other imitative, as different styles of speech. Thus phenomena of space, namely interdialectal or interlingual isoglosses, especially isophones, may be projected into the framework of a single dialect, social or even individual.

The same statement, *mutatis mutandis*, may be made about the time factor in language, particularly in the phonemic field. Any sound change in progress is a synchronic fact. Both the start and the finish of a change coexist for a certain length of time. If the change differentiates the younger generation from the older, there is always some intercourse between the two generations, and the receiver belonging to one is accustomed to decode messages from a sender of the other. Furthermore, the initial and the final stage may co-occur in the use of one and the same generation as two stylistic levels: on the one hand, a more conservative and conventional, on the other, a more fashionable way of talking. Thus synchronic analysis must encompass linguistic changes and, vice versa, linguistic changes may be comprehended only in the light of synchronic analysis.

The decisive factor in phonemic changes and in the diffusion of phonemic phenomena is the shift in the code. The interpretation of events in time and space is primarily concerned with the question: in what respect is the structure of the code affected by such shifts. The motor and physical aspects of these innovations cannot be treated as self-sufficient agents, but must be subjected to the strictly linguistic analysis of their role in the coding system.

Written in 1955 and revised in 1966-1967 by R. Jakobson and M. Halle for the new wording of their outline in the *Manual of Phonetics*, ed. by B. Malmberg, North-Holland Publishing Co., Amsterdam, 1968.

SELECTED LIST OF STUDIES IN GENERAL PHONOLOGY
(TILL 1966)

ALARCOS LLORACH, E., 1961. Fonología española. 3rd ed., Madrid.

ANDRADE, M. J., 1936. "Some questions of fact and policy concerning phonemes", Language *12*.

AVANESOV, R. I., 1955. "Kratčajšaja zvukovaja edinica v sostave slova i morfemy", Voprosy grammatičeskogo stroja. Moscow.

AXMANOVA, O. S., 1966. Fonologija, morfonologija, morfologija. Moscow.

BELARDI, W., 1959. Elementi di fonologia generale. Rome.

BELARDI, W., and N. MINISSI, 1962. Dizionario di fonologia. Rome.

BENVENISTE, É., 1966. Problèmes de linguistique générale. Paris, 119-123.

BERNŠTEJN, S. I., 1962. "Osnovnye ponjatija fonologii", Voprosy jazykoznanija, *11*, No. 5.

BLOCH, B., 1948. "A set of postulates for phonemic analysis", Language *24*.

BLOOMFIELD, L., 1933. Language. New York. Chs. 5-8.

BONFANTE, G., and M. L. P. GERNIA, 1964. Cenni di fonètica e di fonemàtica. Turin.

BUYSSENS, E., 1949. "Mise au point de quelques notions fondamentales de la phonologie", Cahiers Ferdinand de Saussure, *8*.

CHAO, Y. R., 1934. "The non-uniqueness of phonemic solutions of phonetic systems", Academica Sinica, Institute of History and Philology, Bulletin *4*.

CHERRY, E. C., 1956. "R. Jakobson's 'distinctive features' as the normal coordinates of a language", For Roman Jakobson. The Hague.

CHOMSKY, N., 1964. Current issues in linguistic theory. The Hague.

COSERIU, E., 1962. Teoría del lenguaje y lingüística general. Madrid.

DIXON, R. M. W., 1965. Mbabaram phonology. Transactions Philol. Soc.

FANT, C. G. M., 1960. Acoustic theory of speech production. Mouton and Co., The Hague.

FANT, C. G. M., 1966. "Theory of distinctive features", Speech Transmission Laboratory K.T.H., Quart. Rept.

FIRTH, J. R., 1957. Papers in linguistics. London.

FISCHER-JØRGENSEN, E., 1949. "Remarques sur les principes de l'analyse phonémique", Trav. du Cercle Linguistique de Copenhague 5, 231.
FISCHER-JØRGENSEN, E., 1952. "On the definition of phoneme categories on a distributional basis", Acta linguistica 7.
FISCHER-JØRGENSEN, E., 1956. "The commutation test and its application to phonemic analysis", For Roman Jakobson, Mouton and Co., The Hague.
FREI, H., 1952. "Langue, parole et différenciation", Journal de Psychologie.
FRIES, C. C. and K. L. PIKE, 1949. "Coexistent phonemic systems", Language 25.
DE GROOT, A. W., 1940. "Neutralisation d'oppositions", Neophilologus, 25.
HALLE, M., 1954. "The strategy of phonemics", Word, 10.
HALLE, M., 1959. The sound pattern of Russian. Mouton and Co., The Hague.
HALLE, M., 1964. "On the bases of phonology; Phonology in generative grammar", in: The Structure of Language (ed. Fodor/Katz). Prentice Hall Inc. Englewood Cliffs, N.J.
HARRIS, Z. S., 1955. "From phoneme to morpheme", Language, 31.
HARRIS, Z. S., 1960. Structural linguistics. Chicago.
HATTORI, SHIRO, 1961. Gengo gaku no Hoho (Methods in Linguistics). Tokyo.
HJELMSLEV, L., 1938. "Über die Beziehungen der Phonetik zur Sprachwissenschaft", Archiv für vergleichende Phonetik, 2.
HJELMSLEV, L., 1953. Prolegomena to a theory of language. Indiana Univ. Publ. in Anthropology and Linguistics 8. Bloomington, Indiana.
HOCKETT, C. F., 1955. A manual of phonology. Indiana Univ. Publ. in Anthropology and Linguistics 11. Bloomington, Indiana.
IVIĆ, M., 1965. Trends in linguistics. The Hague.
JAKOBSON, R., 1962. Selected writings, I: Phonological studies. Mouton and Co. The Hague.
JAKOBSON, R., C. G. M. FANT, and M. HALLE, 1963. Preliminaries to speech analysis. 4th ed., Cambridge, Mass.
JONES, D., 1962. The phoneme: its nature and use. 2nd ed., Cambridge.
JUILLAND, A. G., 1953. "A bibliography of diachronic phonemics", Word, IX, pp. 198-208.
LAMB, S. M., 1966. "Prolegomena to a theory of phonology". Language 42.
LEPSCHY, G. C., 1966. La linguistica strutturale. Turin.
LYONS, J., 1962. "Phonemic and non-phonemic phonology", I.J.A.L. 28.
MALMBERG, B., 1963. Structural linguistics and human communication. Springer Verlag, Berlin-Göttingen-Heidelberg.
MALMBERG, B., 1964. New Trends in Linguistics. Stockholm-Lund.
MARTINET, A., 1965. La linguistique synchronique. Paris.
MATTOSO, CAMARA, J., 1959. Principios di linguistica general. 2nd ed., Rio de Janeiro. Chs. 2-3.
MILEWSKI, T., 1949. "Derywacja fonologiczna", Biuletyn Polskiego Towarzystwa Językoznawczego 9.
MULJAČIĆ, Ž., 1964. Opca fonologija i fonologija suvremenog talijanskog jexika. Zagreb.
PIKE, K. L., 1947a. "Grammatical prerequisites to phonemic analysis", Word 3.
PIKE, K. L., 1947b. Phonemics. A technique for reducing languages to writing. Ann Arbor, Michigan.

PIKE, K. L., 1952. "More on grammatical prerequisites", Word 8.
PIKE, K. L., 1955. Language in relation to a unified theory of the structure of human behavior. 2nd ed., The Hague.
PILCH, H., 1964. Phonemtheorie 1, Basel.
PIOTROVSKIJ, R. G., 1966. Modelirowanie fonologičeskix sistem i metody ix sravnenija. Moscow-Leningrad.
POS, H. J., 1938. Phonologie en betekenisleer, Meded. Kon. Akad. v. Wetensch. Afd. Letterk. 1, no. 13.
REFORMATSKIJ, A. A., 1955. "O sootnošenii fonetiki i grammatiki", Voprosy grammatičeskogo stroja. Moscow.
ROMPORTL, M., 1963. "Zur akustischen Struktur der distinktiven Merkmale", Z. Phonetik 16.
SAPIR, E., 1949. Selected writings, Berkeley and Los Angeles, pp. 7-60.
SEIDEL, E., 1943. Das Wesen der Phonologie. Bucharest-Copenhagen.
SOTAVALTA, A., 1936. "Die Phonetik und ihre Beziehungen zu den Grenzwissenschaften", Annales Academiae Scientiarum Fennicae 31, No. 3.
SWADESH, M., 1934. "The phonemic principle", Language 10.
ŠAUMJAN, S. K., 1962. Problemy teoretičeskoj fonologii. Moscow.
ŠAUMJAN, S. K., 1965. Strukturnaja lingvistika. Moscow.
Travaux du Cercle Linguistique de Copenhague, 1949. 5 – Recherches structurales.
Travaux du Cercle Linguistique de Prague, 1931. 4 – Réunion phonologique internationale tenue à Prague; 1939. 8 – Études phonologiques, dédiées à la mémoire de N. S. Trubetzkoy.
TRNKA, B., 1954. "Určování fonému", Acta Universitatis Carolinae.
TRUBETZKOY, N. S., 1939. Principes de phonologie (Paris, 1949). German text: Gründzuge der Phonologie = Travaux du Cercle Linguistique de Prague, 3rd ed., Göttingen 1962. French translation with additional studies, Paris, 1949.
TWADDELL, W. F., 1935. On defining the phoneme, Supplement to Language, 16.
UNGEHEUER, G., 1959. "Das logistische Fundament binärer Phonemklassifikationen", Studia Linguistica 13, No. 2.
VACHEK, J., 1964. A Prague school reader in linguistics. Bloomington, Indiana.
WIJK, N. VAN, 1939. Phonologie: een hoofdstuk uit de structurele taalwetenschap. Martinus Nijhoff, The Hague.
WITTING, C., 1959. Physical and functional aspects of speech sounds. Uppsala-Wiesbaden.
ZWIRNER, E., 1938. "L'opposition phonologique et la variation des phonemes", Archiv für vergleichende Phonetik, II.
ZWIRNER, E., 1939. "Phonologie und Phonetik", Acta Linguistica, 1.
ZWIRNER, E., 1964. "Die Beziehungen der Phonemtheorie Trubetzkoys zur Phonetik", Wiener Slavistisches Jahrbuch 11.
ŽINKIN, N. I., 1958. Mexanizmy reči. Moscow.

PART II

TWO ASPECTS OF LANGUAGE AND TWO TYPES OF APHASIC DISTURBANCES

BY

ROMAN JAKOBSON

1. THE LINGUISTIC PROBLEMS OF APHASIA

If aphasia is a language disturbance, as the term itself suggests, then any description and classification of aphasic syndromes must begin with the question of what aspects of language are impaired in the various species of such a disorder. This problem, which was approached long ago by Hughlings Jackson,[1] cannot be solved without the participation of professional linguists familiar with the patterning and functioning of language.

To study adequately any breakdown in communications we must first understand the nature and structure of the particular mode of communication that has ceased to function. Linguistics is concerned with language in all its aspects – language in operation, language in drift,[2] language in the nascent state, and language in dissolution.

At present there are psychopathologists who assign a high importance to the linguistic problems involved in the study of language disturbances;[3] some of these questions have been touched upon in the best recent treatises on aphasia.[4] Yet, in most cases,

---

[1] Hughlings Jackson, Papers on affections of speech (reprinted and commented by H. Head), *Brain*, XXXVIII (1915).

[2] E. Sapir, *Language* (New York, 1921), Chapter VII: "Language as a historical product; drift."

[3] See, for instance, the discussion on aphasia in the Nederlandsche Vereeniging voor Phonetische Wetenschappen, with papers by the linguist J. van Ginneken and by two psychiatrists, F. Grewel and V. W. D. Schenk, *Psychiatrische en Neurologische Bladen*, XLV (1941), p. 1035ff.; cf. furthermore, F. Grewel, "Aphasie en linguistiek", *Nederlandsch Tijdschrift voor Geneeskunde*, XCIII (1949), p. 726ff.

[4] A. R. Luria, *Travmatičeskaja afazija* (Moscow, 1947); Kurt Goldstein, *Language and Language Disturbances* (New York, 1948); André Ombredane, *L'aphasie et l'élaboration de la pensée explicite* (Paris, 1951).

this valid insistence on the linguist's contribution to the investigation of aphasia is still ignored. For instance, a new book, dealing to a great extent with the complex and intricate problems of infantile aphasia, calls for a coordination of various disciplines and appeals for cooperation to otolaryngologists, pediatricians, audiologists, psychiatrists, and educators; but the science of language is passed over in silence, as if disorders in speech perception had nothing whatever to do with language.[5] This omission is the more deplorable since the author is Director of the Child Hearing and Aphasia Clinics at Northwestern University, which counts among its linguists Werner F. Leopold, by far the best American expert on child language.

Linguists are also reponsible for the delay in undertaking a joint inquiry into aphasia. Nothing comparable to the minute linguistic observations of infants of various countries has been performed with respect to aphasics. Nor has there been any attempt to reinterpret and systematize from the point of view of linguistics the multifarious clinical data on diverse types of aphasia. That this should be true is all the more surprising in view of the fact that, on the one hand, the amazing progress of structural linguistics has endowed the investigator with efficient tools and methods for the study of verbal regression and, on the other, the aphasic disintegration of the verbal pattern may provide the linguist with new insights into the general laws of language.

The application of purely linguistic criteria to the interpretation and classification of aphasic facts can substantially contribute to the science of language and language disturbances, provided that linguists remain as careful and cautious when dealing with psychological and neurological data as they have been in their traditional field. First of all, they should be familiar with the technical terms and devices of the medical disciplines dealing with aphasia; then, they must submit the clinical case reports to thorough linguistic analysis; and, further, they should themselves work with aphasic patients in order to approach the cases directly and not only

---

[5]   H. Myklebust, *Auditory Disorders in Children* (New York, 1954).

through a reinterpretation of prepared records which have been quite differently conceived and elaborated.

There is one level of aphasic phenomena where amazing agreement has been achieved during the last twenty years between those psychiatrists and linguists who have tackled these problems, namely the disintegration of the sound pattern.[6] This dissolution exhibits a time order of great regularity. Aphasic regression has proved to be a mirror of the child's acquisition of speech sounds: it shows the child's development in reverse. Furthermore, comparison of child language and aphasia enables us to establish several laws of implication. The search for this order of acquisitions and losses and for the general laws of implication cannot be confined to the phonemic pattern but must be extended also to the grammatical system. Only a few preliminary attempts have been made in this direction, and these efforts deserve to be continued.[7]

---

[6] The aphasic impoverishment of the sound pattern has been observed and discussed by the linguist Marguerite Durand together with the psychopathologists Th. Alajouanine and A. Ombredane (in their joint work *Le syndrome de désintégration phonétique dans l'aphasie*, Paris, 1939) and by R. Jakobson (the first draft, presented to the International Congress of Linguists at Brussels in 1939 – see N. Trubetzkoy, *Principes de phonologie*, Paris, 1949, pp. 317-79 – was later developed into an outline, "Kindersprache, Aphasie und allgemeine Lautgesetze", *Uppsala Universitets Årsskrift*, 1942:9; both papers are reprinted in *Selected Writings*, I, The Hague, 1962, 328-401).

[7] A joint inquiry into certain grammatical disturbances was undertaken at the Bonn University Clinic by a linguist, G. Kandler, and two physicians, F. Panse and A. Leischner: see their report, *Klinische und sprachwissenschaftliche Untersuchungen zum Agrammatismus* (Stuttgart, 1952).

2. THE TWOFOLD CHARACTER OF LANGUAGE

Speech implies a SELECTION of certain linguistic entities and their COMBINATION into linguistic units of a higher degree of complexity. At the lexical level this is readily apparent: the speaker selects words and combines them into sentences according to the syntactic system of the language he is using; sentences in their turn are combined into utterances. But the speaker is by no means a completely free agent in his choice of words: his selection (except for the rare case of actual neology) must be made from the lexical storehouse which he and his addressee possess in common. The communication engineer most properly approaches the essence of the speech event when he assumes that in the optimal exchange of information the speaker and the listener have at their disposal more or less the same "filing cabinet of *prefabricated* representations": the addresser of a verbal message selects one of these "preconceived possibilities" and the addressee is supposed to make an identical choice from the same assembly of "possibilities already, foreseen and provided for".[8] Thus the efficiency of a speech event demands the use of a common code by its participants.

"'Did you say *pig* or *fig?*' said the Cat. 'I said *pig,*' replied Alice."[9] In this peculiar utterance the feline addressee attempts to recapture a linguistic choice made by the addresser. In the common code of the Cat and Alice, i.e. in spoken English, the difference between a stop and a continuant, other things being equal, may change the

---

[8] D. M. MacKay, "In search of basic symbols", *Cybernetics, Transactions of the Eighth Conference* (New York, 1952), p. 183.
[9] Lewis Carroll, *Alice's Adventures in Wonderland*, Chapter VI.

meaning of the message. Alice had used the distinctive feature stop
vs. continuant, rejecting the latter and choosing the former of the
two opposites; and in the same act of speech she combined this
solution with certain other simultaneous features, using the
gravity and the tenseness of /p/ in contradistinction to the acuteness
of /t/ and to the laxness of /b/. Thus all these attributes have been
combined into a bundle of distinctive features, the so-called
phoneme. The phoneme /p/ was then followed by the phonemes
/i/ and /g/, themselves bundles of simultaneously produced distinctive features. Hence the CONCURRENCE of simultaneous entities and
the CONCATENATION of successive entities are the two ways in which
we speakers combine linguistic constituents.

Neither such bundles as /p/ or /f/ nor such sequences of bundles
as /pig/ or /fig/ are invented by the speaker who uses them. Neither
can the distinctive feature stop vs. continuant nor the phoneme
/p/ occur out of context. The stop feature appears in combination
with certain other concurrent features, and the repertory of combinations of these features into phonemes such as /p/, /b/, /t/,
/d/, /k/, /g/, etc. is limited by the code of the given language. The
code sets limitations on the possible combinations of the phoneme
/p/ with other following and/or preceding phonemes; and only part
of the permissible phoneme-sequences are actually utilized in the
lexical stock of a given language. Even when other combinations
of phonemes are theoretically possible, the speaker, as a rule, is
only a word-user, not a word-coiner. When faced with individual
words, we expect them to be coded units. In order to grasp the
word *nylon* one must know the meaning assigned to this vocable
in the lexical code of modern English.

In any language there exist also coded word-groups called
phrasewords. The meaning of the idiom *how do you do* cannot be
derived by adding together the meanings of its lexical constituents;
the whole is not equal to the sum of its parts. Word-groups which
in this respect behave like single words are a common but nonetheless
only marginal case. In order to comprehend the overwhelming
majority of word-groups, we need be familiar only with the constituent words and with the syntactical rules of their combination.

Within these limitations we are free to put words in new contexts. Of course, this freedom is relative, and the pressure of current clichés upon our choice of combinations is considerable. But the freedom to compose quite new contexts is undeniable, despite the relatively low statistical probability of their occurrence.

Thus, in the combination of linguistic units there is an ascending scale of freedom. In the combination of distinctive features into phonemes, the freedom of the individual speaker is zero: the code has already established all the possibilities which may be utilized in the given language. Freedom to combine phonemes into words is circumscribed; it is limited to the marginal situation of word coinage. In forming sentences with words the speaker is less constrained. And finally, in the combination of sentences into utterances, the action of compulsory syntactical rules ceases, and the freedom of any individual speaker to create novel contexts increases substantially, although again the numerous stereotyped utterances are not to be overlooked.

Any linguistic sign involves two modes of arrangement.

(1) COMBINATION. Any sign is made up of constituent signs and/ or occurs only in combination with other signs. This means that any linguistic unit at one and the same time serves as a context for simpler units and/or finds its own context in a more complex linguistic unit. Hence any actual grouping of linguistic units binds them into a superior unit: combination and contexture are two faces of the same operation.

(2) SELECTION. A selection between alternatives implies the possibility of substituting one for the other, equivalent to the former in one respect and different from it in another. Actually, selection and substitution are two faces of the same operation.

The fundamental role which these two operations play in language was clearly realized by Ferdinand de Saussure. Yet of the two varieties of combination – concurrence and concatenation – it was only the latter, the temporal sequence, which was recognized by the Geneva linguist. Despite his own insight into the phoneme as a set of concurrent distinctive features (*éléments différentiels des phonèmes*), the scholar succumbed to the traditional belief in the linear character of language "*qui exclut la possibilité de prononcer deux éléments à la fois*".[10]

In order to delimit the two modes of arrangement which we have described as combination and selection, F. de Saussure states that the former "is *in presentia*: it is based on two or several terms jointly present in an actual series", whereas the latter "connects terms *in absentia* as members of a virtual mnemonic series". That is to say, selection (and, correspondingly, substitution) deals with entities conjoined in the code but not in the given message, whereas, in the case of combination, the entities are conjoined in both, or only in the actual message. The addressee perceives that the given utterance (message) is a COMBINATION of constituent parts (sentences, words, phonemes, etc.) SELECTED from the repository of all possible constituent parts (the code). The constituents of a context are in a state of CONTIGUITY, while in a substitution set signs are linked by various degrees of SIMILARITY which fluctuate between the equivalence of synonyms and the common core of antonyms.

These two operations provide each linguistic sign with two sets of INTERPRETANTS, to utilize the effective concept introduced by Charles Sanders Peirce:[11] there are two references which serve to interpret the sign – one to the code, and the other to the context, whether coded or free, and in each of these ways the sign is related to another set of linguistic signs, through an ALTERNATION in the former case and through an ALIGNMENT in the latter. A given significative unit may be replaced by other, more explicit signs of the same code, whereby its general meaning is revealed, while its contextual meaning is determined by its connection with other signs within the same sequence.

The constituents of any message are necessarily linked with the code by an internal relation and with the message by an external relation. Language in its various aspects deals with both modes of relation. Whether messages are exchanged or communication

---

[10]   F. de Saussure, *Cours de linguistique générale*, 2nd ed. (Paris, 1922), pp. 68f. and 170f.
[11]   C. S. Peirce, *Collected Papers*, II and IV (Cambridge, Mass., 1932, 1934) – see Index of subjects.

proceeds unilaterally from the addresser to the addressee, there must be some kind of contiguity between the participants of any speech event to assure the transmission of the message. The separation in space, and often in time, between two individuals, the addresser and the addressee, is bridged by an internal relation: there must be a certain equivalence between the symbols used by the addresser and those known and interpreted by the addressee. Without such an equivalence the message is fruitless: even when it reaches the receiver it does not affect him.

3. SIMILARITY DISORDER

It is clear that speech disturbances may affect in varying degrees the individual's capacity for combination and selection of linguistic units, and indeed the question of which of these two operations is chiefly impaired proves to be of far-reaching significance in describing, analyzing, and classifying the diverse forms of aphasia. This dichotomy is perhaps even more suggestive than the classical distinction (not discussed in this paper) between EMISSIVE and RECEPTIVE aphasia, indicating which of the two functions in speech exchange, the encoding or the decoding of verbal messages, is particularly affected.

Head attempted to classify cases of aphasia into definite groups,[12] and to each of these varieties he assigned "a name chosen to signify the most salient defect in the management and comprehension of words and phrases" (p. 412). Following this device, we distinguish two basic types of aphasia – depending on whether the major deficiency lies in selection and substitution, with relative stability of combination and contexture; or conversely, in combination and contexture, with relative retention of normal selection and substitution. In outlining these two opposite patterns of aphasia, I shall utilize mainly Goldstein's data.

For aphasics of the first type (selection deficiency), the context is the indispensable and decisive factor. When presented with scraps of words or sentences, such a patient readily completes them. His speech is merely reactive: he easily carries on conversation, but has difficulties in starting a dialogue; he is able to reply to a

[12] H. Head, *Aphasia and Kindred Disorders of Speech*, I (New York, 1926).

real or imaginary addresser when he is, or imagines himself to be, the addressee of the message. It is particularly hard for him to perform, or even to understand, such a closed discourse as the monologue. The more his utterances are dependent on the context, the better he copes with his verbal task. He feels unable to utter a sentence which responds neither to the cue of his interlocutor nor to the actual situation. The sentence "it rains" cannot be produced unless the utterer sees that it is actually raining. The deeper the utterance is embedded in the verbal or non-verbalized context, the higher are the chances of its successful performance by this class of patients.

Likewise, the more a word is dependent on the other words of the same sentence and the more it refers to the syntactical context, the less it is affected by the speech disturbance. Therefore words syntactically subordinated by grammatical agreement or government are more tenacious, whereas the main subordinating agent of the sentence, namely the subject, tends to be omitted. As long as beginning is the patient's main difficulty, it is obvious that he will fail precisely at the starting point, the cornerstone of the sentence-pattern. In this type of language disturbance, sentences are conceived as elliptical sequels to be supplied from antecedent sentences uttered, if not imagined, by the aphasic himself, or received by him from the other partner in the colloquy, actual if not imaginary. Key words may be dropped or superseded by abstract anaphoric substitutes.[13] A specific noun, as Freud noticed, is replaced by a very general one, for instance *machin, chose* in the speech of French aphasics.[14] In a dialectal German sample of "amnesic phasia" observed by Goldstein (p. 246ff.), *Ding* 'thing' or *Stückel* 'piece' were substituted for all inanimate nouns, and *überfahren* 'perform' for verbs which were identifiable from the context or situation and therefore appeared superfluous to the patient.

Words with an inherent reference to the context, like pronouns and pronominal adverbs, and words serving merely to construct

[13] Cf. L. Bloomfield, *Language* (New York, 1933), Chapter XV: Substitution.
[14] S. Freud, *On Aphasia* (London, 1953), p. 22.

the context, such as connectives and auxiliaries, are particularly prone to survive. A typical utterance of a German patient, recorded by Quensel and quoted by Goldstein (p. 302), will serve as illustration:

"Ich bin doch hier unten, na wenn ich gewesen bin ich wees nicht, we das, nu wenn ich, ob das nun doch, noch, ja: Was Sie her, wenn ich, och ich weess nicht, we das hier war ja..."

Thus only the framework, the connecting links of communication, is spared by this type of aphasia at its critical stage.

In the theory of language, since the early Middle Ages, it has repeatedly been asserted that the word out of context has no meaning. The validity of this statement is, however, confined to aphasia, or, more exactly, to one type of aphasia. In the pathological cases under discussion an isolated word means actually nothing but 'blab'. As numerous tests have disclosed, for such patients two occurrences of the same word in two different contexts are mere homonyms. Since distinctive vocables carry a higher amount of information than homonyms, some aphasics of this type tend to supplant the contextual variant of one word by different terms, each of them specific for the given environment. Thus Goldstein's patient never uttered the word *knife* alone, but, according to its use and surroundings, alternately called the knife *pencil-sharpener*, *apple-parer*, *bread-knife*, *knife-and-fork* (p. 62); so that the word *knife* was changed from a free form, capable of occurring alone, into a bound form.

"I have a good apartment, entrance hall, bedroom, kitchen," Goldstein's patient says. "There are also big apartments, only in the rear live bachelors." A more explicit form, the word-group *unmarried people*, could have been substituted for *bachelors*, but this univerbal term was selected by the speaker. When repeatedly asked what a bachelor was, the patient did not answer and was "apparently in distress" (p. 270). A reply like "a bachelor is an unmarried man" or "an unmarried man is a bachelor" would present an equational predication and thus a projection of a substitution set from the lexical code of the English language into the context of the given message. The equivalent terms become two correlated parts of the sentence and consequently are tied by contiguity. The patient was able to select the appropriate term *bachelor* when it was supported by the context of a customary conversation about "bachelor apartments", but was incapable of utilizing the substitution set *bachelor = unmarried man* as the topic of a sentence, because the ability for autonomous selection and substitution had been affected. The equational sentence vainly demanded from the patient carries as its sole information: "'bachelor' means an unmarried man" or "an unmarried man is called 'a bachelor'".

The same difficulty arises when the patient is asked to name an object pointed to or handled by the examiner. The aphasic with a defect in substitution will not supplement the pointing or handling gesture of the examiner with the name of the object pointed to. Instead of saying "this is [called] a pencil", he will merely add an elliptical note about its use: "To write". If one of the synonymic signs is present (as for instance the word *bachelor* or the pointing to the pencil) then the other sign (such as the phrase *unmarried man* or the word *pencil*) becomes redundant and consequently superfluous. For the aphasic, both signs are in complementary distribution: if one is performed by the examiner, the patient will avoid its synonym: "I understand everything" or "Ich weiss es schon" will be his typical reaction. Likewise, the picture of an object will cause suppression of its name: a verbal sign is supplanted by a pictorial sign. When the picture of a compass was presented to a patient of Lotmar's, he responded: "Yes, it's a ... I know what it belongs to, but I cannot recall the technical expression ... Yes ... direction ... to show direction ... a magnet points to the north."[15] Such patients fail to shift, as Peirce would say, from an INDEX or ICON to a corresponding verbal SYMBOL.[16]

Even simple repetition of a word uttered by the examiner seems

---

[15] F. Lotmar, "Zur Pathophysiologie der erschwerten Wortfindung bei Aphasischen", *Schweiz. Archiv für Neurologie und Psychiatrie*, XXXV (1933), p. 104.
[16] C. S. Peirce, "The icon, index and symbol", *Collected papers*, II (Cambridge, Mass., 1932).

to the patient unnecessarily redundant, and despite instructions received he is unable to repeat it. Told to repeat the word"no", Head's patient replied "No, I don't know how to do it." While spontaneously using the word in the context of his answer ("No, I don't ..."), he could not produce the purest form of equational predication, the tautology $a=a$: 'no' is 'no'.

One of the important contributions of symbolic logic to the science of language is its emphasis on the distinction between OBJECT LANGUAGE and METALANGUAGE. As Carnap states, "in order to speak *about* any *object language*, we need a *metalanguage*."[17] On these two different levels of language the same linguistic stock may be used; thus we may speak in English (as metalanguage) about English (as object language) and interpret English words and sentences by means of English synonyms, circumlocutions and paraphrases. Obviously such operations, labeled METALINGUISTIC by the logicians, are not their invention: far from being confined to the sphere of science, they prove to be an integral part of our customary linguistic activities. The participants in a dialogue often check whether they are using the same code. "Do you follow me? Do you see what I mean?" the speaker asks, or the listener himself breaks in with "What do you mean?" Then, by replacing the questionable sign with another sign from the same linguistic code, or with a whole group of code signs, the sender of the message seeks to make it more accessible to the decoder.

The interpretation of one linguistic sign through other, in some respect homogeneous, signs of the same language, is a metalinguistic operation which also plays an essential role in children's language learning. Recent observations have disclosed what a considerable place talk about language occupies in the verbal behavior of pre-school children.[18] Recourse to meta-language is necessary both for the acquisition of language and for its normal functioning.

---

[17] R. Carnap, *Meaning and Necessity* (Chicago, 1947), p. 4.
[18] See the remarkable studies of A. Gvozdev: "Nabljudenija nad jazykom malen'kix detej", *Russkij jazyk v sovetskoj škole* (1929); *Usvoenie rebenkom zvukovoj storony russkogo jazyka* (Moscow, 1948); and *Formirovanie u rebenka grammatičeskogo stroja russkogo jazyka* (Moscow, 1949).

The aphasic defect in the "capacity of naming" is properly a loss of metalanguage. As a matter of fact, the examples of equational predication sought in vain from the patients cited above, are metalinguistic propositions referring to the English language. Their explicit wording would be: "In the code that we use, the name of the indicated object is 'pencil'"; or "In the code we use, the word 'bachelor' and the circumlocution 'unmarried man' are equivalent."

Such an aphasic can neither switch from a word to its synonyms or circumlocutions, nor to its HETERONYMS, i.e. equivalent expressions in other languages. Loss of bilingualism and confinement to a single dialectal variety of a single language is a symptomatic manifestation of this disorder.

According to an old but recurrent bias, a single individual's way of speaking at a given time, labeled IDIOLECT, has been viewed as the only concrete linguistic reality. In the discussion of this concept the following objections were raised:

Everyone, when speaking to another person, tries, deliberately or involuntarily, to hit upon a common vocabulary: either to please or simply to be understood or, finally, to bring him out, he uses the terms of his addressee. There is no such thing as private property in language: everything is socialized. Verbal exchange, like any form of intercourse, requires at least two communicators, and idiolect proves to be a somewhat perverse fiction.[19]

This statement needs, however, one reservation: for an aphasic who has lost the capacity for code switching, the "idiolect" indeed becomes the sole linguistic reality. As long as he does not regard another's speech as a message addressed to him in his own verbal pattern, he feels, as a patient of Hemphil and Stengel expressed it: "I can hear you dead plain but I cannot get what you say ... I hear your voice but not the words ... It does not pronounce itself."[20]

[19] "Results of the Conference of Anthropologists and Linguists", *Indiana University Publications in Anthropology and Linguistics*, VIII (1953), p. 15.
[20] R. E. Hemphil and E. Stengel, "Pure word deafness", *Journal of Neurology and Psychiatry*, III (1940), pp. 251-62.

He considers the other's utterance to be either gibberish or at least in an unknown language.

As noted above, it is the external relation of contiguity which unites the constituents of a context, and the internal relation of similarity which underlies the substitution set. Hence, for an aphasic with impaired substitution and intact contexture, operations involving similarity yield to those based on contiguity. It could be predicted that under these conditions any semantic grouping would be guided by spatial or temporal contiguity rather than by similarity. Actually Goldstein's tests justify such an expectation: a female patient of this type, when asked to list a few names of animals, disposed them in the same order in which she had seen them in the zoo; similarly, despite instructions to arrange certain objects according to color, size, and shape, she classified them on the basis of their spatial contiguity as home things, office materials, etc. and justified this grouping by a reference to a display window where "it does not matter what the things are", i.e. they do not have to be similar (pp. 61f., 263ff.). The same patient was willing to name the primary hues – red, yellow, green, and blue – but declined to extend these names to the transitional varieties (p. 268f.), since, for her, words had no capacity to assume additional, shifted meanings associated by similarity with their primary meaning.

One must agree with Goldstein's observation that patients of this type "grasped the words in their literal meaning but could not be brought to understand the metaphoric character of the same words" (p. 270). It would, however, be an unwarranted generalization to assume that figurative speech is altogether incomprehensible to them. Of the two polar figures of speech, metaphor and metonymy, the latter, based on contiguity, is widely employed by aphasics whose selective capacities have been affected. *Fork* is substituted for *knife*, *table* for *lamp*, *smoke* for *pipe*, *eat* for *toaster*. A typical case is reported by Head:

When he failed to recall the name for "black", he described it as "What you do for the dead"; this he shortened to "dead" (I, p. 198).

Such metonymies may be characterized as projections from the line of a habitual context into the line of substitution and selection: a sign (e.g. *fork*) which usually occurs together with another sign (e.g. *knife*) may be used instead of this sign. Phrases like "knife and fork", "table lamp", "to smoke a pipe", induced the metonymies *fork, table, smoke*; the relation between the use of an object (toast) and the means of its production underlies the metonymy *eat* for *toaster*. "When does one wear black?" – "When mourning the dead": in place of naming the color, the cause of its traditional use is designated. The escape from sameness to contiguity is particularly striking in such cases as Goldstein's patient who would answer with a metonymy when asked to repeat a given word and, for instance, would say *glass* for *window* and *heaven* for *God* (p. 280).

When the selective capacity is strongly impaired and the gift for combination at least partly preserved, then CONTIGUITY determines the patient's whole verbal behavior, and we may designate this type of aphasia SIMILARITY DISORDER.

4. CONTIGUITY DISORDER

From 1864 on it was repeatedly pointed out in Hughlings Jackson's pioneer contributions to the modern study of language and language disturbances:

It is not enough to say that speech consists of words. It consists of words referring to one another in a particular manner; and, without a proper interrelation of its parts, a verbal utterance would be a mere succession of names embodying no proposition (p. 66).[21]

Loss of speech is the loss of power to propositionize... Speechlessness does not mean entire wordlessness (p. 114).[22]

Impairment of the ability to PROPOSITIONIZE, or, generally speaking, to combine simpler linguistic entities into more complex units, is actually confined to one type of aphasia, the opposite of the type discussed in the preceding chapter. There is no WORDLESSNESS, since the entity preserved in most of such cases is the WORD, which can be defined as the highest among the linguistic units compulsorily coded, i.e., we compose our own sentences and utterances out of the word stock supplied by the code.

This contexture-deficient aphasia, which could be termed CONTIGUITY DISORDER, diminishes the extent and variety of sentences. The syntactical rules organizing words into higher units are lost; this loss, called AGRAMMATISM, causes the degeneration of the sentence into a mere "word heap", to use Jackson's image.[23] Word

[21] H. Jackson, "Notes on the physiology and pathology of the nervous system" (1868), *Brain*, XXXVIII (1915), pp. 65-71.

[22] H. Jackson, "On affections of speech from disease of the brain" (1879), *Brain*, XXXVIII (1915), pp. 107-29.

[23] H. Jackson, "Notes on the physiology and pathology of language" (1866), *Brain*, XXXVIII (1915), pp. 48-58.

order becomes chaotic; the ties of grammatical coordination and subordination, whether concord or government, are dissolved. As might be expected, words endowed with purely grammatical functions, like conjunctions, prepositions, pronouns, and articles, disappear first, giving rise to the so-called "telegraphic style", whereas in the case of similarity disorder they are the most resistant. The less a word depends grammatically on the context, the stronger is its tenacity in the speech of aphasics with a contiguity disorder and the earlier it is dropped by patients with a similarity disorder. Thus the "kernel subject word" is the first to fall out of the sentence in cases of similarity disorder and, conversely, it is the least destructible in the opposite type of aphasia.

The type of aphasia affecting contexture tends to give rise to infantile once-sentence utterances and one-word sentences. Only a few longer, stereotyped, "ready made" sentences manage to survive. In advanced cases of this disease, each utterance is reduced to a single one-word sentence. While contexture disintegrates, the selective operation goes on. "To say what a thing is, is to say what it is like", Jackson notes (p. 125). The patient confined to the substitution set (once contexture is deficient) deals with similarities, and his approximate identifications are of a metaphoric nature, contrary to the metonymic ones familiar to the opposite type of aphasics. *Spyglass* for *microscope*, or *fire* for *gaslight* are typical examples of such QUASI-METAPHORIC EXPRESSIONS, as Jackson termed them, since, in contradistinction to rhetoric or poetic metaphors, they present no deliberate transfer of meaning.

In a normal language pattern, the word is at the same time both a constituent part of a superimposed context, the SENTENCE, and itself a context superimposed on ever smaller constituents, MORPHEMES (minimum units endowed with meaning) and PHONEMES. We have discussed the effect of contiguity disorder on the combination of words into higher units. The relationship between the word and its constituents reflects the same impairment, yet in a somewhat different way. A typical feature of agrammatism is the abolition of inflection: there appear such unmarked categories as the infinitive in the place of diverse finite verbal forms, and in languages with declension, the nominative instead of all the oblique cases. These defects are due partly to the elimination of government and concord, partly to the loss of ability to dissolve words into stem and desinence. Finally, a paradigm (in particular a set of grammatical cases such as *he – his – him*, or of tenses such as *he votes – he voted*) present the same semantic content from different points of view associated with each other by contiguity; so there is one more impetus for aphasics with a contiguity disorder to dismiss such sets.

Also, as a rule, words derived from the same root, such as *grant – grantor – grantee* are semantically related by contiguity. The patients under discussion are either inclined to drop the derivative words, or the combination of a root with a derivational suffix and even a compound of two words become irresolvable for them. Patients who understood and uttered such compounds as *Thanksgiving* or *Battersea*, but were unable to grasp or to say *thanks* and *giving* or *batter* and *sea*, have often been cited. As long as the sense of derivation is still alive,. so that this process is still used for creating innovations in the code, one can observe a tendency towards oversimplification and automatism: if the derivative word constitutes a semantic unit which cannot be entirely inferred from the meaning of its components, the GESTALT is misunderstood. Thus the Russian word *mokr-ica* signifies 'wood-louse', but a Russian aphasic interpreted it as 'something humid', especially 'humid weather', since the root *mokr-* means 'humid' and the suffix *-ica* designates a carrier of the given property, as in *nelépica* 'something absurd', *svetlíca* 'light room', *temnica* 'dungeon' (literally 'dark room').

When, before World War II, phonemics was the most controversial area in the science of language, doubts were expressed by some linguists as to whether phonemes really play an autonomous part in our verbal behavior. It was even suggested that the meaningful (SIGNIFICATIVE) units of the linguistic code, such as morphemes or rather words, are the minimal entities with which we actually deal in a speech event, whereas the merely DISTINCTIVE units, such as phonemes, are an artificial construct to facilitate the scientific description and analysis of a language. This view, which was stigmatized by Sapir as "the reverse of realistic",[24] remains, however, perfectly valid with respect to a certain pathological type: in one variety of aphasia, which sometimes has been labeled "atactic", the word is the sole linguistic unity preserved. The patient has only an integral, indissolvable image of any familiar word, and all other sound sequences are either alien and inscrutable to him, or he merges them into familiar words by disregarding their phonetic deviations. One of Goldstein's patients "perceived some words, but ... the vowels and consonants of which they consisted were not perceived" (p. 218). A French aphasic recognized, understood, repeated, and spontaneously produced the word *café* 'coffee' or *pavé* 'roadway', but was unable to grasp, discern, or repeat such nonsensical sequences as *féca, faké, kéfa, pafé*. None of these difficulties exists for a normal French-speaking listener as long as the sound-sequences and their components fit the French phonemic pattern. Such a listener may even apprehend these sequences as words unknown to him but plausibly belonging to the French vocabulary and presumably different in meaning, since they differ from each other either in the order of their phonemes or in the phonemes themselves.

If an aphasic becomes unable to resolve the word into its phonemic constituents, his control over its construction weakens, and perceptible damage to phonemes and their combinations easily follows. The gradual regression of the sound pattern in aphasics regularly reverses the order of children's phonemic acquisitions. This regression involves an inflation of homonyms and a decrease of vocabulary. If this twofold – phonemic and lexical – disablement progresses further, the last residues of speech are one-phoneme, one-word, one-sentence utterances: the patient relapses into the initial phases of infant's linguistic development or even to the pre-lingual stage: he faces *aphasia universalis*, the total loss of the power to use or apprehend speech.

The separateness of the two functions – one distinctive and the other significative – is a peculiar feature of language as compared to

[24] E. Sapir, "The psychological reality of phonemes", *Selected Writings* (Berkeley and Los Angeles, 1949), p. 46ff.

other semiotic systems. There arises a conflict between these two levels of language when the aphasic deficient in contexture exhibits a tendency to abolish the hierarchy of linguistic units and to reduce their scale to a single level. The last level to remain is either a class of significative values, the word, as in the cases touched upon, or a class of distinctive values, the phoneme. In the latter case the patient is still able to identify, distinguish, and reproduce phonemes, but loses the capacity to do the same with words. In an intermediate case, words are identified, distinguished, and reproduced; according to Goldstein's acute formulation, they "may be grasped as known but not understood" (p. 90). Here the word loses its normal significative function and assumes the purely distinctive function which normally pertains to the phoneme.

5. THE METAPHORIC AND METONYMIC POLES

The varieties of aphasia are numerous and diverse, but all of them lie between the two polar types just described. Every form of aphasic disturbance consists in some impairment, more or less severe, either of the faculty for selection and substitution or for combination and contexture. The former affliction involves a deterioration of metalinguistic operations, while the latter damages the capacity for maintaining the hierarchy of linguistic units. The relation of similarity is suppressed in the former, the relation of contiguity in the latter type of aphasia. Metaphor is alien to the similarity disorder, and metonymy to the contiguity disorder.

The development of a discourse may take place along two different semantic lines: one topic may lead to another either through their similarity or through their contiguity. The METAPHORIC way would be the most appropriate term for the first case and the METONYMIC way for the second, since they find their most condensed expression in metaphor and metonymy respectively. In aphasia one or the other of these two processes is restricted or totally blocked – an effect which makes the study of aphasia particularly illuminating for the linguist. In normal verbal behavior both processes are continually operative, but careful observation will reveal that under the influence of a cultural pattern, personality, and verbal style, preference is given to one of the two processes over the other.

In a well-known psychological test, children are confronted with some noun and told to utter the first verbal response that comes into their heads. In this experiment two opposite linguistic predilections are invariably exhibited: the response is intended either as a substitute for, or as a complement to, the stimulus. In the latter case the stimulus and the response together form a proper syntactic construction, most usually a sentence. These two types of reaction have been labeled SUBSTITUTIVE and PREDICATIVE.

To the stimulus *hut* one response was *burnt out*; another, *is a poor little house*. Both reactions are predicative; but the first creates a purely narrative context, while in the second there is a double connection with the subject *hut*: on the one hand, a positional (namely, syntactic) contiguity, and on the other a semantic similarity.

The same stimulus produced the following substitutive reactions: the tautology *hut*; the synonyms *cabin* and *hovel*; the antonym *palace*, and the metaphors *den* and *burrow*. The capacity of two words to replace one another is an instance of positional similarity, and, in addition, all these responses are linked to the stimulus by semantic similarity (or contrast). Metonymical responses to the same stimulus, such as *thatch litter*, or *poverty*, combine and contrast the positional similarity with semantic contiguity.

In manipulating these two kinds of connection (similarity and contiguity) in both their aspects (positional and semantic) – selecting, combining, and ranking them – an individual exhibits his personal style, his verbal predilections and preferences.

In verbal art the interaction of these two elements is especially pronounced. Rich material for the study of this relationship is to be found in verse patterns which require a compulsory PARALLELISM between adjacent lines, for example in Biblical poetry or in the Finnic and, to some extent, the Russian oral traditions. This provides an objective criterion of what in the given speech community acts as a correspondence. Since on any verbal level – morphemic, lexical, syntactic, and phraseological – either of these two relations (similarity and contiguity) can appear – and each in either of two aspects, an impressive range of possible configurations is created. Either of the two gravitational poles may prevail. In Russian lyrical songs, for example, metaphoric constructions predominate, while in the heroic epics the metonymic way is preponderant.

In poetry there are various motives which determine the choice between these alternants. The primacy of the metaphoric process in the literary schools of romanticism and symbolism has been repeatedly acknowledged, but it is still insufficiently realized that it is the predominance of metonymy which underlies and actually predetermines the so-called 'realistic' trend, which belongs to an intermediary stage between the decline of romanticism and the rise of symbolism and is opposed to both. Following the path of contiguous relationships, the realist author metonymically digresses from the plot to the atmosphere and from the characters to the setting in space and time. He is fond of synecdochic details. In the scene of Anna Karenina's suicide Tolstoj's artistic attention is focused on the heroine's handbag; and in *War and Peace* the synecdoches "hair on the upper lip" and "bare shoulders" are used by the same writer to stand for the female characters to whom these features belong.

The alternative predominance of one or the other of these two processes is by no means confined to verbal art. The same oscillation occurs in sign systems other than language.[25] A salient example from the history of painting is the manifestly metonymical orientation of cubism, where the object is transformed into a set of synecdoches; the surrealist painters responded with a patently metaphorical attitude. Ever since the productions of D. W. Griffith, the art of the cinema, with its highly developed capacity for changing the angle, perspective, and focus of 'shots', has broken with the tradition of the theater and ranged an unprecedented variety of synecdochic 'close-ups' and metonymic 'set-ups' in general. In such motion pictures as those of Charlie Chaplin and Eisenstein,[26] these devices in turn were overlayed by a novel, metaphoric "montage" with its "lap dissolves" – the filmic similes.[27]

[25] I ventured a few sketchy remarks on the metonymical turn in verbal art ("Pro realizm u mystectvi", *Vaplite*, Kharkov, 1927, No. 2; "Randbemerkungen zur Prosa des Dichters Pasternak", *Slavische Rundschau*, VII, 1935), in painting ("Futurizm," *Iskusstvo*, Moscow, Aug. 2, 1919), and in motion pictures ("Úpadek filmu", *Listy pro umění a kritiku*, I, Prague, 1933), but the crucial problem of the two polar processes awaits a detailed investigation.
[26] Cf. his striking essay "Dickens, Griffith, and We": S. Eisenstein, *Izbrannye stat'i* (Moscow, 1950), p. 153ff.
[27] Cf. B. Balazs, *Theory of the Film* (London, 1952).

The bipolar structure of language (or other semiotic systems) and, in aphasia, the fixation on one of these poles to the exclusion of the other require systematic comparative study. The retention of either of these alternatives in the two types of aphasia must be confronted with the predominance of the same pole in certain styles, personal habits, current fashions, etc. A careful analysis and comparison of these phenomena with the whole syndrome of the corresponding type of aphasia is an imperative task for joint research by experts in psychopathology, psychology, linguistics, poetics, and SEMIOTIC, the general science of signs. The dichotomy discussed here appears to be of primal significance and consequence for all verbal behavior and for human behavior in general.[28]

To indicate the possibilities of the projected comparative research, we choose an example from a Russian folktale which employs parallelism as a comic device: "Thomas is a bachelor; Jeremiah is unmarried" (*Fomá xólost; Erjóma neženát*). Here the predicates in the two parallel clauses are associated by similarity: they are in fact synonymous. The subjects of both clauses are masculine proper names and hence morphologically similar, while on the other hand they denote two contiguous heroes of the same tale, created to perform identical actions and thus to justify the use of synonymous pairs of predicates. A somewhat modified version of the same construction occurs in a familiar wedding song in which each of the wedding guests is addressed in turn by his first name and patronymic: "Gleb is a bachelor; Ivanovič is unmarried." While both predicates here are again synonyms, the relationship between the two subjects is changed: both are proper names denoting the same man and are normally used contiguously as a mode of polite address.

In the quotation from the folktale, the two parallel clauses refer to two separate facts, the marital status of Thomas and the similar

[28] For the psychological and sociological aspects of this dichotomy, see Bateson's views on "progressional" and "selective integration" and Parsons' on the "conjunction-disjunction dichotomy" in child development: J. Ruesch and G. Bateson, *Communication, the Social Matrix of Psychiatry* (New York, 1951), pp. 183ff.; T. Parsons and R. F. Bales, *Family, Socialization and Interaction Process* (Glencoe, 1955), pp. 119f.

status of Jeremiah. In the verse from the wedding song, however, the two clauses are synonymous: they redundantly reiterate the celibacy of the same hero, splitting him into two verbal hypostases.

The Russian novelist Gleb Ivanovič Uspenskij (1840-1902) in the last years of his life suffered from a mental illness involving a speech disorder. His first name and patronymic, *Gleb Ivanovič*, traditionally combined in polite intercourse, for him split into two distinct names designating two separate beings: Gleb was endowed with all his virtues, while Ivanovič, the name relating a son to his father, became the incarnation of all Uspenskij's vices. The linguistic aspect of this split personality is the patient's inability to use two symbols for the same thing, and it is thus a similarity disorder. Since the similarity disorder is bound up with the metonymical bent, an examination of the literary manner Uspenskij had employed as a young writer takes on particular interest. And the study of Anatolij Kamegulov, who analyzed Uspenskij's style, bears out our theoretical expectations. He shows that Uspenskij had a particular penchant for metonymy, and especially for synecdoche, and that he carried it so far that "the reader is crushed by the multiplicity of detail unloaded on him in a limited verbal space, and is physically unable to grasp the whole, so that the portrait is often lost."[29]

To be sure, the metonymical style in Uspenskij is obviously prompted by the prevailing literary canon of his time, late nineteenth-century 'realism'; but the personal stamp of Gleb Ivanovič made his pen particularly suitable for this artistic trend in its extreme manifestations and finally left its mark upon the verbal aspect of his mental illness.

A competition between both devices, metonymic and metaphoric,

---

[29] A. Kamegulov, *Stil' Gleba Uspenskogo* (Leningrad, 1930), pp. 65, 145. One of such disintegrated portraits cited in the monograph: "From underneath an ancient straw cap, with a black spot on its visor, peeked two braids resembling the tusks of a wild boar; a chin, grown fat and pendulous, had spread definitively over the greasy collar of the calico dicky and lay in a thick layer on the coarse collar of the canvas coat, firmly buttoned at the neck. From underneath this coat to the eyes of the observer protruded massive hands with a ring which had eaten into the fat finger, a cane with a copper top, a significant bulge of the stomach, and the presence of very broad pants, almost of muslin quality, in the wide bottoms of which hid the toes of the boots."

is manifest in any symbolic process, be it intrapersonal or social. Thus in an inquiry into the structure of dreams, the decisive question is whether the symbols and the temporal sequences used are based on contiguity (Freud's metonymic "displacement" and synecdochic "condensation") or on similarity (Freud's "identification and symbolism").[30] The principles underlying magic rites have been resolved by Frazer into two types: charms based on the law of similarity and those founded on association by contiguity. The first of these two great branches of sympathetic magic has been called "homoeopathic" or "imitative", and the second, "contagious magic".[31] This bipartition is indeed illuminating. Nonetheless, for the most part, the question of the two poles is still neglected, despite its wide scope and importance for the study of any symbolic behavior, especially verbal, and of its impairments. What is the main reason for this neglect?

Similarity in meaning connects the symbols of a metalanguage with the symbols of the language referred to. Similarity connects a metaphorical term with the term for which it is substituted. Consequently, when constructing a metalanguage to interpret tropes, the researcher possesses more homogeneous means to handle metaphor, whereas metonymy, based on a different principle, easily defies interpretation. Therefore nothing comparable to the rich literature on metaphor[32] can be cited for the theory of metonymy. For the same reason, it is generally realized that romanticism is closely linked with metaphor, whereas the equally intimate ties of realism with metonymy usually remain unnoticed. Not only the tool of the observer but also the object of observation is responsible for the preponderance of metaphor over metonymy in scholarship. Since poetry is focused upon the sign, and pragmatical prose primarily upon the referent, tropes and figures were studied mainly as poetic devices. The principle of similarity underlies poetry; the metrical parallelism of lines, or the phonic equivalence

---

[30]   S. Freud, *Die Traumdeutung*, 9th ed. (Vienna, 1950).
[31]   J. G. Frazer, *The Golden Bough: A study in Magic and Religion*, Part I, 3rd ed. (Vienna, 1950), chapter III.
[32]   C. F. P. Stutterheim, *Het begrip metaphoor* (Amsterdam, 1941).

of rhyming words prompts the question of semantic similarity and contrast; there exist, for instance, grammatical and anti-grammatical but never agrammatical rhymes. Prose, on the contrary, is forwarded essentially by contiguity. Thus, for poetry, metaphor, and for prose, metonymy is the line of least resistance and, consequently, the study of poetical tropes is directed chiefly toward metaphor. The actual bipolarity has been artificially replaced in these studies by an amputated, unipolar scheme which, strikingly enough, coincides with one of the two aphasic patterns, namely with the contiguity disorder.